BLACK MUSIC IN AMERICA

BLACK MUSIC IN AMERICA

A HISTORY THROUGH ITS PEOPLE

JAMES HASKINS

Illustrated with photographs

Thomas Y. Crowell   New York

Black Music in America
Text copyright © 1987 by James Haskins
Copyright © 1987 by James Haskins
All rights reserved. No part of this book may be
used or reproduced in any manner whatsoever without
written permission except in the case of brief quotations
embodied in critical articles and reviews. Printed in
the United States of America. For information address
Thomas Y. Crowell Junior Books, 10 East 53rd Street,
New York, N.Y. 10022. Published simultaneously in
Canada by Fitzhenry & Whiteside Limited, Toronto.
Designed by Trish Parcell Watts
10 9 8 7 6 5 4 3 2 1
First Edition

Library of Congress Cataloging-in-Publication Data
Haskins, James, 1941–
   Black music in America.

   Summary: Surveys the history of black music in America,
from early slave songs through jazz and the blues to soul,
classical music, and current trends.
   1. Afro-Americans—Music—History and criticism—
Juvenile literature.   2. Music—United States—History
and criticism—Juvenile literature.   [1. Afro-Americans
—Music—History and criticism.   2. Music—History and
criticism]   I. Title.
ML3556.H33 1987   781.7'296073   85-47885
ISBN 0-690-04460-7
ISBN 0-690-04462-3 (lib. bdg.)

ACKNOWLEDGMENTS

I am grateful to Miss Leontyne Price, Mr. Charles Davis, and Mr. Bo Diddley for taking the time to talk with me, to Elizabeth Gordon for her enthusiasm and foresight, and to Gina Heiserman for her enthusiasm and superb editing. Thanks also to Ann Kalkhoff and Kathy Benson for their help.

CONTENTS

BLACK MUSIC IN AMERICA

CHAPTER 1

THEY CAME AGAINST THEIR WILL

EARLY SLAVE MUSIC

They came in chains, brought to the New World as slaves. They did not immigrate, seeking greater opportunity, like others who came to America. They were seized from their villages and homes and not allowed to take any possessions with them—no favorite piece of clothing or kitchen utensil or handmade musical instrument. But they did have their songs, and they would re-create their instruments and their music to keep their hearts and souls alive through nearly two hundred fifty years of slavery in the New World.

By the time slavery was abolished, most of them would not go back to Africa, for Africa was no longer their home. America

1

was. Despite their poor treatment, the land and the culture had become part of them. And in spite of the fact that most white Americans at the time did not consider blacks to be their equals, whites had taken into their own hearts certain elements of black culture. By the time the slaves were emancipated, they had given to America not just the sweat of their brows and the strength of their backs, but the seeds of the first truly American cultural gift to the world—American music.

In the more than one hundred years since then, the influence of black music on American popular music, not to mention on popular music and culture around the world, has been incalculable. Blues, jazz, rock 'n' roll—all these musical forms originated with blacks. And white performers and groups—from Benny Goodman to Frank Sinatra to the Beatles to Rod Stewart to Boy George—have said that they owe their biggest debt to black music. Three hundred fifty years ago, who would have thought that the poor, helpless slaves aboard ships from Africa would bring such a powerful legacy with them to the new land?

Many of these slaves left no record at all of their lives. In fact, in the South, it was not until around World War II that the births of black babies were recorded systematically. Officially, blacks were all but invisible, defined more by laws that denied them their rights than by laws that guaranteed their rights. There was a time during slavery when they were even denied the right to make their own music, and for many years after that, white promoters and performers collected the lion's share of profits from black music. Meanwhile, whites didn't think that blacks were capable of singing or playing white music.

Without the stubborn efforts of blacks to show that they could play white music, some of the distinctively black forms that make up American music never would have enjoyed a wide audience. Without the courageous work of blacks to show that distinctively black music should be as celebrated as white music, some of the most important American musical styles would not have developed at all.

This is a history of black music in America through the lives of black people who made it. It focuses on the innovators and pioneers; on the black people who showed they could make white music, thus opening up new paths for black performers in general, as well as on the black people who made black music. It is as much a history of obstacles overcome as of the blossoming and branching out of new musical forms.

In the early 1800s, a slave-ship captain named Theodore Canot described how the slaves kept their music alive even as they journeyed to unknown fates in the New World: "During afternoons of serene weather, men, women, girls, and boys are allowed while on deck to unite in African melodies which they always enhance by extemporaneous *tom-tom* on the bottom of a tub or tin kettle."

While Canot probably didn't think about it, this was one of the only ways the slaves could unite in their sorrow and fear, for they did not often share a common language. The slaves who arrived at the African slave markets came from tribes all over Africa, and they were thrown together in the slave ships without regard for tribe or language. In fact, slave-ship captains made a point of *not* putting slaves from the same tribes together, for if the slaves had been able to talk with

3

one another, they also might have been able to plan revolts. The same was true of slave owners in the New World. It was in their best interests that slaves not be able to communicate with one another.

These slave-ship captains and slave owners did not understand that the slaves were able to communicate with one another quite well through their music. Through their songs, the slaves shared the rhythms of their sorrow and their fear and their hopelessness. Through the rhythms of their makeshift drums, they communicated their calls to rebellion. Between 1699 and 1845, there were at least fifty-five revolts aboard slave ships. Most of them failed, but they caused enough trouble and damage to make the insurance companies that wrote policies for slave ships offer a special form of coverage against insurrections aboard slave ships. The most famous successful revolt occurred aboard the *Amistad*, an American clipper ship, in 1839. Bound for Cuba, the ship was taken over by slaves led by a man named Cinque, who changed course and headed for the United States, finally landing off New London, Connecticut. The slaves were taken into custody by American officials and sat through two federal trials to determine their status under United States and international law. Former President John Quincy Adams defended them, and in 1841 they were able to return to Africa.

Other slaves died during the voyages, for on many slave ships they were packed close together in narrow bunks below deck, chained together, and denied the food and sanitary facilities necessary for life. Some committed suicide by throwing themselves overboard. Those who reached the New World and were sold in the coastal slave markets to southern plantation owners and northern businessmen continued to rely on their music—their songs and their drums—both to communicate with one another and to keep their morale intact.

For some time, slave masters did not realize that the drums the slaves made from hollowed-out logs or nail kegs, with animal skins tightly stretched over one end, were being used for communication. They thought the slaves were just making their African music. They knew these drum sounds carried far, even to the next plantation, but it didn't occur to them that the drumbeats were a sort of "Morse code" the slaves used to make plans for revolts or escapes. Yet they knew that slaves on different plantations were somehow communicating with each other. There were too many revolts and escapes.

When it finally became clear to the slave masters that the drums were being used as a form of communication, drums were outlawed. But that didn't stop the slaves from keeping the drumbeat alive. Instead, they used their feet.

Back in Africa, in the absence of drums, some tribes had used their heels to tap out rhythms on the sun-baked clay. In the New World, slaves did the same thing on the floors of their huts or the boards of their dancing floors. As recently as 1942, a white woman named Lydia Parrish described the sound still being made in McIntosh County, Georgia: "It always rouses my admiration to see the way in which the McIntosh County 'shouters' tap their heels on the resonant board floor to imitate the beat of the drum their forbears were not allowed to have," she wrote. "Those who hear the records of the musical chants which accompany the ring-shout . . . cannot believe that a drum is not used, though how the effect is achieved with the heels alone—when they barely leave the floor—remains a puzzle." There is no way of knowing how many slave revolts or escapes were aided by the "Morse code" of slave heels tapping on wood floors on those southern slave plantations.

It is also likely that the slaves learned to give double meaning to the religious songs they sang. Quite a few Negro spirituals contain messages that white slave masters did not suspect and certainly did not anticipate when they decided that their slaves should be converted to Christianity. The slaves embraced Christianity. In Louisiana, which had first been settled by the Spanish and the French, they converted to Catholicism. In Virginia, South Carolina, Alabama, and Georgia, settled first by the English, the Methodist and Baptist churches were strong, and since they allowed much singing in their services, the slaves were able to incorporate their own love of song into their newfound faiths. Out of this mingling of slave culture and Protestant culture came the songs called spirituals, which were the first great black musical gift to America. They were often called sorrow songs, because they expressed the deep suffering the slaves endured and their yearnings for the peaceful kingdom of heaven.

But the songs were also a way for the slaves to communicate with each other—to plan meetings, to help escaped slaves, and to remind one another that there was hope for freedom. The spiritual "Deep River," for example, was sung to announce a meeting at the river:

> *Deep river*
> *My home is over Jordan, yes*
> *Deep river, Lord,*
> *I want to cross over into camp ground.*

When a slave had run away and the master had discovered his absence, the other slaves on the plantation might sing "Wade in the Water." Slaves on neighboring plantations would hear the song and take it up, and the runaway, wherever he was, would know that he should take to the river so the bloodhounds would not be able to follow his scent:

Wade in the water, wade in the water.
Children, God going to trouble the water.

It is no accident that, after the Underground Railroad began, slaves in the South took to singing a spiritual called "The Gospel Train." The Underground Railroad was a route from the South to Canada and freedom, a route marked by homes that would take in runaways and provide them with places to sleep, food, clothing, and help in traveling to the next "station." Part of the spiritual went,

The gospel train is coming
I hear it just at hand—
I hear the car wheels moving,
And—rumbling thro' the land.
Get on board—children,
Get on board.

While it is interesting to think about how the slaves used their drums and drumlike sounds and their spirituals to work against their masters and for their own freedom, most of the music of the slaves was not used in that way. Mostly, the slaves used music to make their burdens lighter, to restore their spirits when they were drained of courage, and to enjoy the little free time they had.

When the slaves labored, they sang work songs. They made up songs about picking cotton, and harvesting sugarcane, and loading and unloading ships on the docks. In this, they were not very different from other groups of workers who shared a tradition of music and singing. English and Irish sailors sang sea chanteys as they worked. The slaves had a special form of singing, known as the call-and-response form, that allowed individuals to make up new verses and then to be answered by the group. The group acted like a chorus.

The slaves also used this call-and-response form when they sang their sorrow songs, or spirituals, on Sundays. They would take a plain Methodist hymn and turn it into an entirely new song, one with much more rhythm and depth. Church was often the only outlet for their feelings, both their deep suffering and their great religious joy. During the week, they were under the heel of the master, and they had to keep their emotions in check. But in church, they could let out all those pent-up emotions, and by singing together they could share those emotions and gain solace in their togetherness. At those southern slave religious services on Sundays, the voices could be heard for miles around, and the rhythms and intonations were like nothing the local whites had ever heard before.

The slaves also introduced new instruments to America. Among the first, besides the drum, were the bones. These were actually animal bones that had been cleaned and allowed to dry white in the sun. When played expertly, they made a wonderful *clackety-clack* sound to accompany the drum or heel rhythms the slaves produced. More familiar to us today is the banjo. In Africa, it is called a *bania* or *banju*. In 1784, Thomas Jefferson wrote about an intriguing instrument used by his slaves that he called a banjar. Made by the slaves, the instrument did not have frets; but it was shaped the same way as banjos are today, and it had strings and was strummed in the same way as banjos.

The white slave owners were intrigued by the slaves' songs and instruments and music. At first, they encouraged the slaves to sing and play (but not beat drums) because they felt that the slaves were happier—and less rebellious—if they were allowed to make their music. But before long, the masters began enjoying the music for its own sake, as the rhythms and songs crept into their souls and set their feet to tapping and their bodies to moving. Generations of white southern children, raised by black women, remembered being sung to sleep with Negro spirituals, and associated them with warmth and security. (Today, there are Negro Spiritual societies in the South whose memberships are exclusively white, made up of people for whom the songs were lullabies.)

What made these southern whites respond to the music made by slaves, whom they otherwise degraded, is complex. For one thing, in the days of slavery, most white Americans were of Anglo-Saxon heritage and did not have a strong musical tradition. They came from a culture that regarded music and dancing and singing as sinful, or at least not very respectable, and that considered most public displays of emotion as poor taste. Their musical forms were very stiff and emotionless by comparison, and there was something about the great emotion and the great variety of rhythms in Negro music that they responded to in spite of themselves. Dr. Alain Locke, who wrote about Negro music in the 1930s, suggested that the most expressive and emotional musical forms in any society come from its lowest class: "As we approach the peasant stocks of the Irish, Italian, German and Russian nations, we see they all have their well-springs of folk music," he wrote. "It has simply been the lot of the Negro in America to be the peasant class, and thus to furnish the sub-soil of our national music."

Plantation masters came to enjoy the music made by plantation slave bands. After a while, performances by these slave bands became part of the entertainment for visiting guests, as did slave dancing. But the whites still looked to Europe for their musical standards, although European music and dancing were generally not as lively. There were Irish jigs and folk songs, to be sure, but these were not considered real dancing and music, just as the dancing and the music of the slaves was not considered really acceptable. They were entertainment, but not to be considered an art form.

If you asked most Americans in those days what was music, they would have mentioned the names of European classical musicians and composers, voices such as the soprano and the baritone, and instruments such as the piano and the violin. If you asked most Americans if they thought a black person could sing or play that kind of music, they would have said no. But the first blacks in America to become famous for their music were trained in the classical European tradition. They became famous *because* they could play or sing "white" music. Still, they are important to the history of black music because they helped to make black musical performers acceptable, and that would eventually lead to greater acceptance of black music.

The blacks who managed to achieve some success in the

world of music in America in the first half of the nineteenth century were primarily women singers of European classical music. Of course, black men could learn European music as well as white men. But American whites were just not comfortable with the idea that black men could be classically trained; that would have made them too close to human. Black women were less threatening, and few whites worried about them demanding to be seen as human. Even so, Elizabeth Taylor Greenfield was in her forties before she enjoyed the opportunity for a major concert debut.

Elizabeth Taylor Greenfield

Elizabeth Taylor Greenfield was born in Natchez, Mississippi, in 1809. Both she and her parents were slaves, but they were lucky to have a mistress, Elizabeth H. Greenfield, who decided to join the Society of Friends (the Quakers) and who took the family with her when she moved to Philadelphia, where the Quakers were headquartered. There, she freed the infant Elizabeth and her parents.

Young Greenfield showed musical prowess early and taught herself to play the guitar. She also studied voice briefly with a local amateur singer named Miss Price. Unfortunately, the Society of Friends frowned on music and singing, and Greenfield realized that she had limited possibilities to develop her talent in Pennsylvania. In 1851, at the age of forty-two, she moved to Buffalo, New York.

That same year, Greenfield made her concert debut as a soprano under the sponsorship of the Buffalo Musical Association. In reviewing the concert, the Buffalo *Commercial Advertiser* dubbed her "The Black Swan." Colonel J. H. Wood, who took over management of her career soon afterward, saw that she was billed as "The Black Swan" during the extensive two-year tour of northern cities that he arranged for her, and she was known by that nickname for the rest of her career.

The range of Greenfield's voice was three and one quarter octaves, and in the rave reviews she received wherever she performed, she was often compared with the foremost white female singers of the day, including "America's Sweetheart," Jenny Lind. Unlike Jenny Lind, however, she was unwelcome in the southern states. The only place left for her to go was to Europe.

On April 6, 1853, Greenfield sailed for England. In London, she studied under George Smart, organist and composer for Queen Victoria's Chapel Royal. She was given money to live on and for her lessons by both Harriet Beecher Stowe, author of *Uncle Tom's Cabin*, the best-selling novel about slavery, and the Duchess of Sutherland. During her months in England, she performed a number of concerts, including a command performance for Queen Victoria at Buckingham Palace.

Returning to the United States, Greenfield performed concerts throughout the North, and with her success in Europe as a credential, she was very popular. At one point in the 1850s, she toured with Thomas Bowers, a first-rate tenor who was called "The Colored Mario" after a famous Italian tenor of the period named Conte di Candia Mario.

The Civil War and her own age eventually ended Greenfield's singing career. The onset of the war brought much musical entertainment to a halt, and by the time the war broke out, she was in her early fifties. She devoted the rest of her life to teaching young black sopranos, hoping that they might follow in her footsteps. Sadly, none of them enjoyed the same success. White America was not ready to welcome very many black achievers, no matter how talented they were. There usually was room for about one per generation. Elizabeth Taylor Greenfield died in Philadelphia in 1876, her performing career having been far too brief. She did have the distinction, however, of being the first black American concert singer to have won acclaim on both sides of the Atlantic.

The Hyers Sisters took over where Elizabeth Taylor Greenfield had left off. Anna and Emmie Louise Hyers were natives of California and did not have the same slave roots as Elizabeth Greenfield. The sisters sang duets: Anna had a high soprano voice, Emmie Louise a voice so deep and wide of range that it was called *tenore*. They made their concert debut in Sacramento, California, in 1867, and four years later made what was billed as a "continental tour" of the U.S. and Canada. They stayed above the Mason-Dixon Line, however. By that time, the Civil War had been fought, and won by the Union, but the South was occupied by Federal troops and was not a welcoming place for black concert singers. The Hyers Sisters enjoyed their greatest triumphs at concerts in such cities as New York, Boston, and Montreal. And, like Elizabeth Taylor Greenfield before them, they were regarded as a novelty. The people who paid to hear them sing marveled that two black sisters could sing classical, operatic music. They regarded the sisters as phenomena—unusual characters, freaks of nature.

And so it follows that the black man most celebrated by whites for his musical genius in that era was a blind man. Like the women, he was not threatening. He was "Blind Tom."

Blind Tom

Thomas Greene was born near Columbus, Georgia, in 1849. He and his mother, Charlotte Wiggins, were slaves belonging to the Oliver family, who later sold Charlotte Wiggins to Colonel James N. Bethune. The baby Tom, being blind and thus of no worth as a potential worker, was "thrown in" with the deal, at no extra cost to Colonel Bethune. Little Tom did not show any unusual musical gifts until he was about seven, but there is evidence that he had them all along. When Tom was about four, Colonel Bethune had bought a piano for his family, and for the next three years the little boy listened as Mrs. Bethune, who had been a music teacher before her marriage, played it and taught her daughters to play. Then one day when Tom was about seven, he sat down at the piano and played with absolute perfection some of the music he had heard the previous day.

Little Tom had two remarkable gifts: a perfect sense of pitch and a phenomenal musical memory. Not only could he re-create any musical piece he heard, but he could also improvise on the piece. That meant that he wasn't just imitating the sounds, but was understanding them as well. Moreover, he understood all types of music. He didn't play only plantation melodies or popular hits of the day—he also played Bach and Beethoven with the best.

Word got around about the blind musical prodigy, and in 1858, when Tom was nine, Colonel Bethune hired him out to a Savannah, Georgia, planter named Perry Oliver. Tom was presented as "the musical prodigy of the age: a Plantation Negro Boy." Oliver made a great deal of money from Blind

Tom's concerts, and while the outbreak of the Civil War in the spring of 1861 may have been one reason Tom went back to Colonel Bethune, another reason may have been that Oliver had decided to keep the profits from Tom's concerts for himself.

After the war, although according to the law of the land he was no longer a slave, Tom remained with the Bethune family, and Colonel Bethune became his legal guardian.

Billed as a "MUSICAL PRODIGY—with Wonder Powers as a Pianist," Blind Tom toured extensively throughout the United States and Canada and had his first formal musical instruction. He also toured in Europe and South America.

Because his musical memory was so unusual, Blind Tom was regarded as something of a freak, and there was often a circuslike atmosphere to his concerts. He was always being challenged to prove that he could remember one composition or another. (And since he claimed to know some seven thousand pieces, that left a lot of room for challenges!) Once, while performing at the White House, he played correctly a twenty-page piece a short time after hearing it. To increase his repertoire still further, Blind Tom's managers hired professional musicians to play new pieces for him. When he performed, his audiences were given a list of more than eighty pieces, including "Classical Selections," "Piano-Forte Solos," "Fantasias and Caprices," "Marches," "Imitations," "Descriptive Music," "Songs," and "Parlor Selections." The audience then got to select the pieces that they wished to hear. People who really knew music, including the leading musicians of the time, were very respectful of Blind Tom, for they recognized that he was a master musician.

15

Long after he had stopped being a child prodigy, Blind Tom gave concert tours. He was so well-known, in fact, that few people had not heard of him. During the 1890s, he was more often billed as a vaudeville attraction than as a concert artist. By that time, Colonel James Bethune had died and James S. Bethune, the colonel's son, had taken over Blind Tom's guardianship and management. After the death of James S. Bethune, his widow, who later married an Albert J. Lerché, enjoyed big profits from Blind Tom's concert tours.

Blind Tom retired in 1898 after more than thirty continuous years on the concert stage, during which he had made fortunes for his various guardians and managers. Six years later, in answer to frequent rumors in the press about his death, he made a comeback tour sponsored by Albert J. Lerché. He died in Hoboken, New Jersey, in 1908. A marker at the place on Highway 217A near Columbus, Georgia, where Blind Tom was born, is on the list of national historic landmarks.

There were many fine musicians and singers in the South, but very few of them ever got the opportunity to display their skills beyond the borders of their own plantations or local areas. In the United States before the Civil War, it was primarily northern blacks, who had either been born free or somehow secured their freedom and moved to the North, who had gained a large audience for their music. Among these were several black bands.

The band was the most common musical group in the 1800s. Marching bands were especially popular, and many of these originated as military bands. Since blacks were not allowed to serve in the military at this time, black musicians did not have the opportunities to come together and form such musical groups, but they still played the same kind of music. There were several highly successful black bands. Of these, the most famous and most long-lasting was Frank Johnson's.

Frank Johnson's Band

Frank Johnson was a native of Philadelphia who showed early musical talent, especially on the trumpet. He was taken on as a protégé by P. S. Gilmore, known as "the bandmaster of America," who taught him the fine points of conducting, arranging, and composing. In 1839, Johnson organized his own band, drawing on the talents of a number of other black Philadelphia musicians. The band, which played in the military style, was so successful that, four years later, it undertook a European concert tour.

The band toured throughout England, Scotland, and Ireland and gave a command performance for Queen Victoria. At these concerts, Frank Johnson himself always played at least one solo on the trumpet. The Queen was so impressed by his performance that she presented him with a silver trumpet.

Sadly, Frank Johnson died young and at the height of his career, in 1846. But he left a lasting legacy in his band, which refused to die with him. It was taken over by Joe Anderson and continued to play throughout the northern half of the United States and in Europe until Anderson's death in 1874. After that, it split into two factions. Both the Excelsior Band and Frank Jones's Orchestra became famous in their own right, not only for their marches, but also for their concert music featuring talented string sections.

*   *   *

These black musicians and singers who became famous in the years when slavery was still legal were honored for their achievements in the popular white music of the time. Music or singing that was distinctly black was still not considered real music by whites. No white promoter would have thought of presenting a concert of spirituals or a banjo recital. Yet these particularly black forms were widely shared by whites. Well before the Civil War, whites had started borrowing from black music to create their own entertainment forms. Minstrelsy was a direct borrowing from blacks, though for a long time whites would not let blacks take part in the minstrel shows.

CHAPTER 2

WAY DOWN SOUTH

BLACK MUSIC GAINS A WIDER AUDIENCE

By 1800, the United States of America had declared itself
independent of the British government, but its people were
still strongly dependent upon British and other European
models for their culture. They looked to Europe for their
modes of dress, their language and reading habits, their painting and sculpture, their theater, and their music. But by the
early 1800s, the very fact that Americans were not the subjects
of Britain or any other European nation had begun to assist
in the creation of truly American cultural forms. The citizens
of the United States were still largely European in their her-

itage, but they were slowly becoming identifiably American, shaping their heritage to their new surroundings. It followed that they would begin to create art and literature and music that were also distinctly American. Black American music helped to influence the creation of two distinctly American musical forms: musical comedy and popular ballads.

Minstrelsy sprang directly from the slave quarters of southern plantations. The white performers in these variety stage shows blackened their faces with burnt cork, played musical instruments such as the banjo and the bones that were associated with blacks, sang songs in imitation of black songs, danced imitations of black dances, and even imitated black language in their comic dialogues. White minstrels made a point of visiting plantations on "research trips" to get new material for their acts by watching plantation bands and performances by slave singers and dancers, noting the clothes the slaves wore, and recording the Pidgin English of the slaves. From about 1830 until the outbreak of the Civil War, minstrelsy enjoyed its golden age. The material was fresh and funny. The imitations of the slaves were not really cruel; in fact, they were rather admiring of the rhythms and humor of the Negro. After the Civil War and emancipation, however, minstrelsy changed. White southerners, who had been chiefly responsible for the creation of minstrelsy, felt bitter toward the former slaves. Their imitations of blacks took on a cruel tone. Harsh stereotypes of blacks, some of which unfortunately still exist today, became set in the public mind at this time: the stupid, shuffling darky, the citified dude, the prostitute. No longer did the minstrels seek out real blacks for material, and as a result there was no new material. Finally, a few black entertainers were allowed into minstrelsy, but by then the form was so rigidly set that they, too, had to put burnt cork on their faces when they performed!

Minstrelsy was primarily a comedy form. Songs and music were secondary to jokes and antics and comedy skits. But minstrelsy was the first truly American contribution to the history of stage entertainment, and it owed its very existence to the Negro. Moreover, some of the most important popularizers of black songs and rhythms, black and white, got their start in minstrelsy.

Among them was Stephen Foster, a white man and a northerner who, ironically, wrote the most memorable songs about the pre–Civil War South. He published some songs that did not borrow from the Negro folk songs he heard, but very few of these were to be lastingly popular; "Jeannie with the Light Brown Hair" is one that was. Foster's major fame came with songs like "Old Folks at Home" (also known as "Swanee River"), "Old Black Joe," "My Old Kentucky Home," and "Way Down South." He once said that he wanted to be "the best Ethiopian songwriter," by which he meant the best songwriter of Negro minstrel songs. (The term "Ethiopian" was used to stand for black or Negro.) To a large extent, Foster succeeded. Not only did he attend minstrel shows, but he also visited Kentucky plantations to hear real Negro plantation singing. Foster created an indelible, sentimental picture of a gracious Old South of peaceful plantations and happy darkies, and was the first real popularizer of black-influenced music. In literature, the white writer Joel Chandler Harris did the same thing with his Uncle Remus stories. At least in the music world, however, there was a little bit of room for a black composer to publish

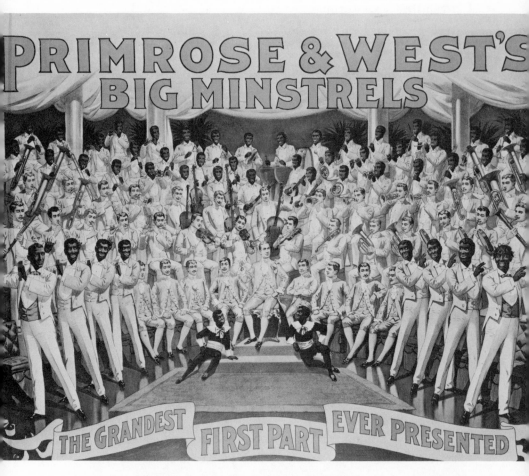

Minstrelsy was rigidly segregated. In the 1890s Primrose and West started sending out troupes of blacks and whites, but in different groups. The only times blacks and whites appeared on the same stage were in posters such as this one. (CULVER PICTURES)

songs in the black tradition. In the world of American literature at that time, black writers did not have the same opportunity. While not as well-known as Stephen Foster, the black composer James Bland has often been compared with him.

James Bland

James Bland also became famous for his sentimental ballads that glorified the Old South, though like Stephen Foster he was born in the North and of middle-class parents who were far away from the slave and Negro folk experience. Of mixed black, white, and Indian parentage, he was born in Flushing, New York, on October 22, 1854, but he grew up primarily in Philadelphia, Pennsylvania, and Washington, D.C. His father, Allan M. Bland, had been one of the first black college graduates in America, but since there were few professions open to a black man, no matter how well educated, Mr. Bland worked as a tailor until James was a teenager.

Bland first became interested in music while the family was in Philadelphia, where they had moved when he was six. The Civil War had ended, and many former slaves had made their way to northern cities such as Philadelphia. They brought their music with them, and young Bland first heard banjo music on the streets of the city. Fascinated by the instrument, he managed to save the money to buy one, and taught himself to play.

In 1868, when Bland was 14, his father finally secured a job that befitted his education. He was appointed to a position in the U.S. Patent Office in the nation's capital, and the family moved to Washington, D.C. James finished high school there and later enrolled at all-black Howard University in Washington. He was supposed to study law, but his heart was in music.

Many former slaves were employed at Howard as groundkeepers and janitors. Bland listened eagerly to their songs and their stories of slavery, and probably spent more time with them than in his classes. Eventually, against his father's wishes, he dropped out of Howard, determined to make his living at music. He got jobs singing and playing for private gatherings and at local hotels, and he began composing songs to expand his repertoire. Like Stephen Foster, his songs were sweet, sentimental ballads. In 1875, when he was about nineteen, he joined a minstrel troupe out of Boston, Massachusetts, called the Original Black Diamonds.

Over the next few years, Bland worked with a variety of blackface minstrel troupes, providing them with a wealth of new music to play and sing. It is said that George Primrose, the most prominent white promoter of minstrel shows, used some of Bland's compositions in his shows, which practically guaranteed Bland's success in minstrelsy.

Around 1880, Bland joined Haverly's Genuine Colored Minstrels. Jack Haverly was already famous for presenting huge whites-in-blackface minstrel shows in America and England. This time, he decided to do the same thing with a troupe composed of real blacks, though they still performed in blackface. Renamed Haverly's European Minstrels, the group opened in London in 1881, and one of the hits of the show was James Bland performing his own composition "O Dem Golden Slippers."

Even after the Haverly troupe dissolved, Bland remained in Europe, which he had found a much more welcoming place than his own country. There, for nearly a decade, he performed *without blackface makeup* in the leading music halls and was extremely popular; in fact, he was known there as "the idol of the music halls." He made a great deal of money—according to legend, he earned ten thousand dollars a year from performing fees and royalties on his songs—and spent it on fashionable clothes and travel.

By the early 1900s, Bland had returned to the United States, where he settled in Washington, D.C., and tried to begin a new career. But musical and entertainment tastes had changed; vaudeville had replaced minstrelsy as the popular entertainment form, and the public was not interested in an aging minstrel. Bland's last work was for a musical show, *The Sporting Girl*, for which he wrote the songs, but the show was not a success. Eventually, he moved back to Philadelphia, where he had first been introduced to the music that had sustained him all his life, but apparently it could no longer sustain him financially. The fabled huge sums in royalties he had once earned slowed to a trickle. When Bland died in 1911 at the age of fifty-six, apparently of a bad cold that turned into pneumonia, he was penniless and alone.

James Bland never stopped composing—in the course of his career, he wrote a total of more than six hundred songs, and during his heyday in Europe, it was said that he turned out a song a week. Of these, the best remembered besides "O Dem Golden Slippers" is "Carry Me Back to Old Virginny," which he copyrighted when he was twenty-four years old. Ironically, most people thought that the song had been composed by Stephen Foster. In 1940, when it became the official Virginia state song, many people were surprised to learn that it had been written by a black man.

Both Stephen Foster and James Bland borrowed elements from Negro folk music—the work songs and the spirituals— but by the time they were finished, the folk elements were mere shadows of themselves. These composers, and others, softened the Negro dialect and the special rhythms. In doing so, they did help to make black folk music more acceptable to whites, but they also left out many of the elements that made the music unique. After the Civil War and emancipation, southern life underwent a radical change, and so did the lives of the slaves. Some of the most beautiful black folk songs might have disappeared if it hadn't been for a group that began its musical career with no intention of singing identifiably black music, but that ended up being the instrument of preservation of many of the finest black spirituals.

The Fisk Jubilee Singers

Fisk University in Nashville, Tennessee, was founded after the Civil War by the Freedmen's Bureau, which was established by the federal government to help the newly emancipated slaves carve out new lives as freedmen. The university opened in 1866, and its purpose was to educate the best and the brightest black youth so that they could make the world a better place for the people of their race. While the Freedmen's Bureau provided the funds to get the university started, it did nothing to keep it going. That was up to the American

Missionary Society, and that group did not have much money for Fisk. By 1871, there was neither heat nor food for the students, and the American Missionary Society was talking about closing down the school.

George L. White, the school's musical director, decided to form a chorus and go on the road giving concerts to raise money for the school. He chose eighteen singers (ten women and eight men), rehearsed with them, and set up a concert date at Oberlin College in Ohio. Oberlin, a progressive, co-educational school founded in 1833, had already graduated several black women and thus would be a fairly welcoming place for the Fisk Jubilee Singers. Still, the venture was a gamble, and Adam K. Spence, principal of Fisk (it was more like a high school than a college in those early days), took a courageous step in giving the group everything in the school's treasury, save one dollar, to finance the trip.

The Jubilee Singers, named in memory of the year of emancipation, which blacks called the jubilee, started out singing current popular songs. They had no intention of singing slave spirituals. "The slave songs . . . were associated with slavery and the dark past, and represented things to be forgotten," wrote Ella Sheppard, a member of the group. "Then, too, they were sacred to our parents who used them in their religious worship and shouted over them." But George White kept encouraging them to sing the spirituals, and after a time, according to Ella Sheppard, "We finally grew willing to sing them privately, and sitting upon the floor . . . we practiced softly, learning from each other the songs of our fathers. We did not dream of ever using them in public. Had Mr. White suggested such a thing, we certainly had [sic] rebelled. After

Some of the Fisk Jubilee Singers. From their dress and posture, it is clear that they did not want to be identified with slave songs or slavery time. (FISK UNIVERSITY)

many months we began to appreciate the wonderful beauty and power of our songs; but continued to sing in public the usual choruses, duets, solos, etc. Occasionally two or three slave songs were sung at the close of the concert. But the demand of the public changed this order. Soon the land rang with our slave songs."

At Oberlin and the other places where they gave their first concerts, the Fisk Jubilee Singers were greeted with polite applause. When they began to introduce a couple of spirituals at the end of their concerts, the applause was enthusiastic. It did not take George White long to figure out that the public, largely white, wanted spirituals, and that the Fisk Jubilee Singers, whose mission was to raise money for their school, should give the public what it wanted. By the time they had been on the road eight months, the group had raised enough money to pay Fisk's debts.

The Jubilee Singers went on a second tour, which included concerts in Brooklyn, New York, at the invitation of Henry Ward Beecher, a Congregationalist minister with national influence. There, they attracted the attention of other influential people, who helped to organize a European tour in 1874. During that first trip to Europe, they sang before Queen Victoria of England and the royal family, members of the British Parliament, and the Czarina of Russia.

Their second European tour lasted three years, from May 1875 to July 1878, and they traveled the European continent, singing for the heads of state of the Netherlands, Germany, and Saxony. What an incredible experience for a group of poor, young blacks! They met people and saw sights that the majority of white Americans would never see. But they never lost sight of their goal: to raise money for their school. In seven years, the Fisk Jubilee Singers raised one hundred fifty thousand dollars, a huge sum for the time.

After that second European tour, Fisk University gave up sponsorship of the Jubilee Singers. The group's success had spawned many imitators, and the university did not feel it could manage the job of arranging the touring when there were so many other groups with which the original Jubilee Singers were being confused. Reorganized as a private group, the singers went on a six-year tour around the world that was not only financially successful for the singers, but good public relations for the university. In fact, most people did not realize that the group was no longer sponsored by Fisk.

By 1898, the university had decided to sponsor a new group of Fisk Jubilee Singers, which lasted until 1911. Between 1911 and 1947, the group was a professional, private group; since 1947, it has been a student group.

The great contribution of the Fisk Jubilee Singers was that they not only brought to the attention of the world the cause of black education, but also brought to the world the spirituals that the members had once been so reluctant to sing in public.

By the time the Fisk Jubilee Singers had completed their second European tour, many European, not to mention American, composers had recognized the exciting new rhythms of black music and come to regard them as the purest American folk music. In 1893, the innovative composer Antonín Dvořák chose American Negro spirituals to represent America in his symphony *From the New World*.

If we seem to be getting ahead of the story by jumping

to the 1890s, it is no accident. Between the end of the Civil War and the 1890s, there was not a lot of black music history being made. It was an in-between period for black Americans. They had to make the adjustment from slavery times to new times. The older people, who had known slavery, kept on singing and playing their music, while the younger people were rather ashamed of the music of their fathers and mothers. Many of these younger people moved away from plantations and rural southern towns and took up residence in the cities, where schools and manufacturing jobs and other opportunities were available. In these cities, two new strains of black music—the blues and ragtime—began to grow, but it would take about twenty years before they developed to the point where they began to have a major impact on American music.

Meanwhile, blacks were just glad to be allowed into the mainstream of American musical entertainment—the minstrel shows, tired and stiff though they had become. Black minstrels, in fact, gave new life to minstrelsy, bringing new material to the form. After a time, the very fact that they were "real Ethiopians" almost guaranteed them some success in minstrelsy.

The vogue for "real Ethiopians" also benefited some performers who were not really in the minstrel vein. They were still primarily black women singers trained in opera. The most famous in the latter part of the century was Sissieretta Jones, who was sort of a successor to Elizabeth Taylor Greenfield and the Hyers Sisters. But unlike her predecessors, she lived in a time when it was possible to branch out into other types of music because white audiences were more welcoming to black performers like her.

Sissieretta Jones—"The Black Patti"

Sissieretta Jones was born Matilda S. Joyner in Portsmouth, Virginia, in 1869, but she grew up in Providence, Rhode Island, where her family moved when she was seven. At an early age, she was singing solos at the Pond Street Baptist Church in Providence and at other local gatherings. Later, she attended the Providence Academy of Music and then the New England Conservatory of Music. Sometime in the 1880s, she also studied in London with a private voice teacher. While still a teenager, she was giving concerts in various New England cities, and when she made her debut in New York in April 1888, three months after her nineteenth birthday, she was identified in the press as "Mme. M. S. Jones, New England's Rising Soprano Star."

At the Bergen Star Concert at Steinway Hall that year, Jones brought down the house, and the next day the New York newspapers gave her headlines. One critic called her "the Black Patti," comparing her with Adelina Patti, a famous white opera singer of the time, and the name stuck. Her manager wanted to take advantage of this great publicity and booked her into the Academy of Music; she sang to large audiences for two nights. Clearly, she was a true operatic discovery, and there was talk of her singing at the Metropolitan Opera House. Two popular operas, *Aïda* and *L'Africaine*, called for "dark" female singers, and "the Black Patti" seemed perfect for the roles. The managers of the Metropolitan actually signed Jones for work at the Opera House, but she never did sing on that stage. A fire closed down the house shortly after she was signed, and kept her out of that premier

American spotlight. Instead, she signed with the Tennessee Concert Company that summer to tour with a large company in the West Indies.

In April 1889, Jones performed in New York City with the Georgia Minstrels, which was hardly the right company for a classically trained soprano. Fortunately, she was soon back on the regular concert stage, and by 1892 was firmly established as a prima donna. She was now billed as Madame M. Sissieretta Jones, and in April of that year she was invited to the White House to sing at a reception held by President and Mrs. Benjamin Harrison in September, 1892. In 1893, she sang at the Pittsburgh Exposition and also at the Chicago World's Fair and gave concerts up and down the eastern seaboard, drawing huge crowds.

In 1893, after some contractual difficulties with her manager, Jones fired him and hired a black manager named Ednorah Nahor. Nahor signed her with the Damrosch Orchestra Company, which sponsored her in tours both in the United States and abroad.

Three years later, Jones made a major change in the direction of her career. She was the featured star in a black vaudeville show called *Black Patti Troubadours*. The show was the idea of two white New York promoters who thought the time was right to present Jones in an all-black show. They hired black composer Bob Cole to write the show, and *Black Patti Troubadours* toured the world for many years. The show followed the then-popular minstrel pattern in a general way: There were comedy sketches and an "olio," or hodgepodge of acts, and "Black Patti" herself did not appear until the finale, which was called the "Operatic Kaleidoscope" and which fea-

tured her in songs and operatic selections with the chorus. Still, Jones was the real drawing card for the show, and it was largely due to her that it was uniquely successful among large, all-black shows in the South. Exactly what qualities made her so popular are hard to define. She was a very beautiful, statuesque woman, with great dignity; and, of course, she had a voice that would have brought *bravas* from audiences at the Metropolitan Opera, had she only been given that chance.

Although Sissieretta Jones was celebrated as the most famous black singer in America for nearly thirty years, she did not break new musical ground. Her music was European operatic music. But like the other black performers before her, she helped pave the way for those musicians who were to perform and create the music of black Americans.

OPPOSITE: *While she was really an opera singer, and was called "the Black Patti" after the white opera singer Adelina Patti, Sissieretta Jones could not get enough work singing opera and had to travel with a minstrel-type show to make a living.*

(MUSEUM OF THE CITY OF NEW YORK)

CHAPTER 3

RAGTIME AND THE BLUES

THE FIRST AGE OF BLACK AMERICAN MUSIC

The forms of minstrelsy were so set, and so powerful, that they influenced even black musicians for many years after the Civil War. The larger public was accustomed to the style of minstrelsy and often demanded it of musicians who traveled alone, making their living by playing in saloons and cabarets in cities along the banks of the Mississippi. It was necessary for these itinerant, or traveling, musicians to bow to public taste in order to make a living; but by the 1880s, they had begun to find a way to break out of the minstrel forms. What they did was adapt the elements of rhythm and swing in minstrelsy to the ragtime form.

Ragtime was music played in "ragged time," which is another way of saying syncopation. It was entirely different from the staid rhythms of European music. It was closer to the rhythms of the black dancers who used their heels to make drum sounds, or to that of the black church singers who could vary the rhythms of a Christian hymn so much that a white Christian could not even recognize it. It was also related to the call-and-response pattern of Negro work songs and to the percussive rhythms of the banjo and the bones.

There is no way to trace exactly when the first ragtime was played on an old upright piano in some Mississippi River saloon, for ragtime was not written down in the early years. But some music historians point to the date 1892, and a composition called "Michigan Waters," published by a New Orleans Negro named Tony Jackson, as the beginning of ragtime. The following year, the word "ragtime" appeared for the first time on a sheet-music cover when Fred Stone, a black musician in Detroit, copyrighted a piece called "Ma Ragtime Baby." Ragtime seemed to burst into the public consciousness in that year of the very first world's fair, the World's Columbian Exposition in Chicago. The exposition gave a number of traveling black musicians an opportunity to hear one another, and what they heard excited them as well as the larger public. For Scott Joplin, his experience at the exposition gave him hope that black music might have a chance at respectability.

Scott Joplin

Scott Joplin was born in Texarkana, Texas, in 1868. Showing an early interest in music, he was lucky to receive training from local black music teachers who taught him the basics of

European classical music. He became something of a celebrity in the Texarkana area, and he determined to make his living at music. In 1888, when he was twenty, he left home to seek his musical fortune.

At that time, a large number of traveling pianists criss-crossed the South and Midwest by train and river steamer, by wagon and foot, performing wherever and whenever they could. Most were concentrated in the Mississippi Valley, in the river towns with their comparatively large populations and established saloon districts. They brought their own musical styles to the Mississippi Valley, and in turn they were influenced by the folk songs and dances and hymns of the people there. Out of this commingling of styles came the peculiar, syncopated kind of piano playing that came to be known as ragtime. It was a form that excited Scott Joplin, and at which he excelled.

Joplin went to Chicago for the World's Columbian Exposition in 1893 because he hoped to get work in one of the many saloons that had sprung up on the fringes of the fairgrounds. He got work, but more important, he got a sense that black music was gaining in stature. Many musicians he met, both black and white, were playing music in ragged time. Also, an all-black revue called *The Creole Show* played a whole season at the fair, and the performers, who were *not* in blackface, emphasized music and dancing rather than jokes and skits. *The Creole Show* was thus a definite departure from the old minstrel patterns.

There in Chicago, Scott Joplin formed his first band, though it soon broke up. He then formed a singing group. In 1895, he had his first two songs published in New York; both were sentimental ballads typical of the time. By the following year, however, he had begun to publish instrumental pieces that showed true ragtime influences.

Feeling that he needed more training in composition, Joplin enrolled at Smith College of Music in Sedalia, Missouri. He supported himself by playing piano in local saloons, but he was convinced that ragtime was a kind of music that could move out of the saloons and into middle-class drawing rooms. All the while, he was composing rags, notating them as carefully as he would have written down a classical music composition. In 1899, his "Maple Leaf Rag" was published. Later, it would become a classic, but at the turn of the century the larger public still did not consider ragtime to be on a par with "better music." Joplin, discouraged that his music was not appreciated the way he thought it should be, said, "Maybe fifty years after I am dead it will be."

Joplin pressed on. He composed a ragtime folk ballet called *The Ragtime Dance* and formed his own Scott Joplin Drama Company to perform it. But no music publisher considered the ballet marketable enough to publish. Joplin's ragtime piano compositions were gaining in popularity, however. By 1900, the invention of the Pianola made ragtime accessible to the average person.

The Pianola was the forerunner of the player piano. It had a mechanism that enabled the piano to play itself. A paper roll was passed over a cylinder containing holes connected to tubes; these tubes, in turn, were connected to the piano action. When a hole in the paper passed over a hole in the cylinder, it caused a current of air to pass through a tube, and this current of air caused the correct piano hammer to strike the correct string. Someone with no musical talent at all could thus "play" a musical piece on a Pianola. Soon, Pianolas were all the rage, and people who could not play a note began to appreciate the syncopated rhythms of ragtime.

Now there was great demand for ragtime piano compositions, and those of Scott Joplin were among the most popular. But Joplin was not content with mere popularity. He wanted his music to be respected. In 1911 he finished another ragtime opera, *Treemonisha*, and spent most of his money in a vain attempt to get it produced. He died depressed and broke in New York in 1917 at the age of forty-nine, still thinking his music was unappreciated.

Some fifty-three years later, the music of Scott Joplin enjoyed a great revival. In 1970, new recordings of his rag compositions were issued. A couple of years later, his piano works were collected and published. In 1975, his ragtime folk opera *Treemonisha* was produced in Houston, Texas; later, it played on Broadway. The previous year, Joplin's grave in St. Michael's Cemetery in Astoria, New York, had finally been marked with a bronze plaque. Joplin had said that his work would not be appreciated until fifty years after his death. If one dates the Joplin revival as beginning in 1970, then he was off by just three years.

While Scott Joplin died without seeing ragtime elevated to the same level as classical music, he did live to see it become commercially popular. By about 1902, the school of ragtime known as Tin Pan Alley had arisen in New York City, primarily because New York was the center of the music publishing business. The "nervous" syncopation of ragtime seemed to fit

By the time this photograph was taken, Scott Joplin's rags were very popular. But what he really wanted was for ragtime music to be respected as much as classical music. (HASKINS COLLECTION)

the hurried tempo of the large and busy city. It was a commercialized style of ragtime—its "tinny" sound gave rise to the name Tin Pan Alley—and was played and written primarily by white men who had learned it from black musicians. Though popular, it was but a few notches above black ragtime in respectability. Also, it broke no new ground. The new and exciting rhythms were still coming out of Memphis and St. Louis and other Mississippi River towns. Among the most exciting were those of a man who became known throughout the world as "the Father of the Blues."

W. C. Handy

William Christopher Handy was born in Florence, Alabama, on November 16, 1873. Both his father and his grandfather were Methodist ministers, and his family considered music and dancing sinful except for the singing and playing of hymns in church. But young Handy loved all kinds of music. As a child, he would sneak away to hear the black laborers singing as they worked loading and unloading cargo along the Tennessee River. Florence and three neighboring cities, including Muscle Shoals, were busy riverside towns, and they were alive with musical influences for a young boy. Muscle Shoals would later host an important recording studio for "down-home blues" music.

Handy taught himself to play the cornet, but at first he did not try to make his living at it. He taught public school for a while and also worked in a foundry. But his heart was in music, and in 1893 he organized a quartet that played its way to the

World's Columbian Exposition in Chicago. While the group did well in Chicago, Handy was a poor manager and the quartet disbanded.

He then got a job with Mahara's Colored Minstrels as bandleader and solo cornettist. Billed as a minstrel group, Handy and his fellow musicians had to follow the old minstrel formulas, and he found himself playing Irish folk songs, Virginia reels, and "coon songs," which were caricatures of Negro folk songs. He also played some classical music, which he liked and performed well. But he missed the chance to play the kind of music that had so excited him as a child—the black work songs and spirituals. One evening in 1897, while the group was on tour in California, Handy decided to include some of that down-home music and played "Georgia Camp Meeting." The audience responded so enthusiastically that Handy decided to form his own band and try to make a success at playing such music.

He formed that band in 1903, in Clarksdale, Mississippi. All the band members wore uniforms, and they played as many dance engagements as they could, for their music was eminently danceable. One time in Cleveland, however, they were challenged to a contest by a ragtag band of three musicians, playing guitar, mandolin, and bass viol, and Handy realized that what his group was playing was not real downhome music at all. The threesome played such exciting music— Handy called it a "backyard wail"—that they got more in tips than Handy and his group got in salary.

After that, Handy realized that he needed to get some new material and that he would have to find it in black folk music. He disbanded his group and went on a search, alone, for that

43

music, hanging around saloons and railroad yards and docks. He was especially interested in the secular sorrow songs he heard: songs that had their origins in early slave laments, but that had undergone a transition along with the lives of the people who sang them. After emancipation, the majority of southern blacks moved from being plantation slaves to being sharecroppers for white landowners. Their sorrow songs were now more likely to be sung by individuals, rather than by groups. The instrument most commonly associated with these songs was now the guitar, though most poor blacks learned on a makeshift instrument far different from what we know today as a guitar. Often, it was a wire taken from the handle of a broom and nailed to a wall, stretched so that it had proper tone. As one hand plucked a beat, the other hand slid a bottle along the surface of the wire to change the pitch. The wall served as a resonator. These one-stringed wall instruments were very similar to instruments common in West Africa and Brazil.

The songs played on these instruments were called the blues. Like the sorrow songs of the earlier plantation slaves, the blues represented the cries of people who had nothing, who seemed to get nothing no matter how hard they tried, and whose lives seemed hopeless. By this time, such songs were often sung in lively rhythms—like laughing to keep from crying.

In 1905 in Memphis, Handy formed another band, which he called the Pythian Band. This time, black folk music was an integral part of the program. Handy arranged all the music and composed two blues pieces, which he tried, unsuccessfully, to get published, although it was his composing that later made W. C. Handy so famous. Having studied for a time at Kentucky Musical College, he had learned how to notate music, and he devised a method for notating the way black folk singers "slurred," or "broke," the third and seventh tones of the musical scale. It was these "suspended" tones that characterized the music that was called the blues.

In 1909, Memphis was the scene of a hotly contested mayoral election. Each candidate hired a local black band to play at street rallies, and Handy's was hired for the campaign of a candidate named Crump. Handy composed a special blues piece for the occasion, called "Mr. Crump" and based on folk songs he had heard. It was a lively tune, and soon everyone in town was singing it. Mr. Crump was elected, due in no small part to that catchy campaign song.

Handy tried to get "Mr. Crump" published, but again he was unsuccessful. Finally, in 1912, he took matters into his own hands and personally financed the publication of his composition "Memphis Blues," which not only contained notations for those "blue notes" that were peculiar to black singing, but also was written in tango rhythm.

The tango rhythm was originally an African rhythm called *tangana*. By the time Handy used it, it had become associated with Spain, but the Spanish had probably gotten it from Africa during the era of the slave trade. It was, and is today, the basic rhythm of Afro-Cuban music and the folk music of Brazil. How Handy discovered that rhythm is not known, but the fact that he used a basically African rhythm, along with the blue notes that were particular to black singing, makes "Memphis Blues" an important composition.

One thousand copies of the sheet music were published, but Handy did not have the resources to advertise his song or to get it played at sheet-music shops. Thus, when a white

Memphis promoter named T. C. Bennett offered to buy all rights to the song for one hundred dollars, Handy, who needed the money, agreed.

Not long afterward, a simplified version of "Memphis Blues," with words added, was published in New York. It became a best-seller, but W. C. Handy received no royalties. When he sought to include the song in his *Blues Anthology* thirteen years later, he was denied permission to do so, for he did not own any rights to it. Tin Pan Alley had taken over his song for the sum of one hundred dollars.

Handy kept on composing. In 1912, the same year that he financed the first publication of "Memphis Blues," he composed "St. Louis Blues," which would also become a classic. He moved to New York City to be near the center of the publishing industry and formed his own music publishing company. Unfortunately, the business went bankrupt, and Handy was forced to sell his house in New York in order to pay off his business debts. He remained loyal to the cause of blues music, however, and in his later years published various anthologies of that music. His autobiography, *Father of the Blues*, was published in 1941, and in 1958, Hollywood released a highly fictionalized film biography called *St. Louis Blues*, starring the popular singer Nat "King" Cole. Handy died that same year, but he was active to the end in keeping alive the blues tradition.

W. C. Handy formed his first band in 1903. Scott Joplin had formed his first band a decade earlier. Many other black musicians and composers were forming their own bands during that first age of black music, 1890–1918. With the end of slavery and the beginning of popular interest in black rhythms,

W. C. Handy devoted his life to creating and popularizing blues music. In his later years, he published several anthologies of blues music. (MUSEUM OF THE CITY OF NEW YORK)

they were finally able to do so. Ernest Hogan, a black vaude-ville artist, and Will Marion Cook, a violinist and composer who wrote some of the first black musical comedies in the 1890s, formed the first genuine black band in 1905. By gen-uine is meant a band that did not rely on the white minstrelsy tradition, but that had arisen out of the genuine black plan-tation music tradition. They called the band the Memphis Students, not because its members were from Memphis, or even students, but because they wanted to pay tribute to the source of their folk style. In fact, they organized the group in New York City from among the best musicians who had grav-itated from all over to that city. The instruments included banjos, mandolins, guitars, saxophones, drums, a violin, one or two brass instruments, and a double bass. The style was syncopated music. Billed as a dance orchestra with solo sing-ers, the group made its debut at Proctor's Theater in New York City and was immediately successful. Like the Fisk Ju-bilee Singers, the Memphis Students clearly represented real black music; and like the Fisk Jubilee Singers, the group soon went to Europe to show the people there what genuine black music was all about. One of the members of the Memphis Students was James Reese Europe, and his experience with the group left a lasting impression on him, for it proved to him that there was a large audience for black music, especially dance music.

James Reese Europe

James Reese Europe was born in Mobile, Alabama, on Feb-ruary 22, 1881, but he grew up in Washington, D.C., where his family moved before he was ten. His mother played the piano and encouraged her children when they showed musical talent. Not only James, but also his sister Mary and his brother John became professional musicians. James got his early formal training in the local public schools, but he later took private violin lessons with Enrico Hurlei, the assistant director of the United States Marine Band.

In 1904, Europe went to New York, where he hoped to get work in one of the musical-show companies that flourished in the city. He played piano in small nightclubs before joining the Memphis Students. Ernest Hogan and Will Marion Cook had a dispute over who was in charge of the Memphis Students, and Europe apparently sided with Cook. By 1906, Europe was alternating with Cook as musical director of the musical comedy shows. That year, he was director of *The Shoofly Regiment*, and in 1909, he directed *Mr. Lode of Koal*, which starred the most famous black vaudevillian, Bert Williams, both on Broadway and on tour. Meanwhile, Europe was watching the number of talented black musicians in New York City increase, along with the popular American taste for dance bands. By 1910, he and others had decided to try to bring the two together.

They organized the Clef Club that year. It functioned both as a union and as a musical contractor, and was the first attempt to organize black musicians. All the members paid dues and in return could be hired out in various combinations as dance bands of three to thirty men. The Clef Club announced itself at a big concert at the Manhattan Casino in October 1910. There were eleven pianos in addition to an assortment of other, largely stringed, instruments, for Europe believed that the pianos gave the background of chords that were typical of black harmony. The concert and the club were immediately

49

James Reese Europe (center) was one of the first to try to organize black musicians, and he conducted many groups before he formed his most famous one, the 369th Infantry Band.

(FRANK DRIGGS COLLECTION)

successful, and within a short time the Clef Club managed to buy a house on West Fifty-third Street to serve as a clubhouse and booking office. While the purpose of the Clef Club was to get bookings for its members, the organization also performed benefit concerts to aid black institutions. In 1912, Europe conducted a 125-piece Clef Club Symphony Orchestra at Carnegie Hall for the benefit of the Music School Settlement for Colored; he conducted a similar benefit concert, also at Carnegie Hall, for the settlement the following year. These concerts were further distinguished by Europe's choice of selections—he made a point of featuring the works of black composers, including his old friend Will Marion Cook's compositions "Swing Along," "Exhortation," and "Rain Song." While audience reaction to these concerts was largely favorable, there were critics in both the white and black communities who felt that Europe's emphasis on black music was too great. Disagreements within the club's membership over how much black music to include eventually led Europe to go his own way.

In 1913, Europe resigned from the Clef Club and formed another organization, the Tempo Club, with similar goals. From the members of that organization, he drew personnel for his Negro Symphony Orchestra, his National Negro Orchestra, Europe's Society Orchestra, and Europe's Double Quintet. All these groups emphasized black rhythms. They were heavy on pianos, as well as on mandolins and banjos, because Europe felt the stringed instruments provided the steady, strumming accompaniment that made the music distinctive. He still received criticism, but he stuck to his particular brand of music. Eileen Southern, in her 1971 book

The Music of Black Americans: A History, quotes him as telling an interviewer: "You see, we colored people have our own music that is part of us. It's the product of our souls; it's been created by the sufferings and miseries of our race. Some of the melodies we played Wednesday were made up by slaves of the old days, and others were handed down from the days before we left Africa. . . . We have developed a kind of symphony music that, no matter what else you think, is different and distinctive, and that lends itself to the playing of the peculiar compositions of our race." The Victor Talking Machine Company apparently agreed, and offered him a recording contract in 1913; it is likely that Europe's bands were the first black bands to make recordings.

Europe's music also lent itself very well to the dances of a white couple named Vernon and Irene Castle, and in 1914 the couple contacted Europe and began an association that was extremely fruitful for all three. The Castles benefited from, and helped to inspire, a dance craze that swept the country at that time. They popularized the fox-trot, the one-step, and the turkey trot, as well as a dance called the Castle walk. Europe composed special music for the dances, and it was he who actually invented both the turkey trot and the fox-trot. Soon, the Castles had their own dance salon in New York City called Castle House or, more frequently, Castles-in-the-Air. Europe and an eleven-piece group consisting of violins, cornets, clarinets, mandolins, drum, and piano were the resident orchestra. In turn, the Castles often appeared in Europe's concerts. Vernon Castle was killed in an airplane accident in 1917, cutting short not only the couple's highly successful career but also their unique collaboration with James Reese Europe.

On April 6 of that same year, the United States declared war on Germany and entered World War I, which had been going on in Europe since July 28, 1914. At that time, there were four black regiments (numbering about ten thousand men) in the regular Army, as well as ten thousand more blacks in various units of the National Guard. Many other blacks began to volunteer for service, and within a single week the quota for black volunteers was filled. Add the black volunteers to the number of blacks who were drafted, and by the end of the war the number of blacks in the armed services had increased tenfold. Most of the black Regular Army units had their own bands, with black bandmasters. The 349th Infantry had one under Norman Scott; the 351st had one under Dorsey Rhodes; the 367th, called "The Buffaloes," under Egbert Thompson; the 368th under Jack Thomas; and the 370th under George Duff. The best-known of these bands were headed by members of the Clef Club—the 350th under J. Tim Brymm and the 807th under Will Vodery. But the best-known of all was the one headed by James Reese Europe—the 369th.

The 369th Infantry Division out of New York, formerly the Fifteenth Infantry Division, was headed by Colonel William Hayward, and Hayward wanted his division's band to be the best. Thus, he asked James Reese Europe to organize it for him. Europe set about doing so, but he soon found that it was impossible to find a group of musicians in New York who would live up to his, and Colonel Hayward's, expectations— the best musicians were, he said, paid too well to give up their positions to play in a military band. So Colonel Hayward contacted a wealthy man named Daniel Gray Reid and got ten thousand dollars for a nationwide recruitment effort. Europe used that money to assemble the finest band he could, bringing in men from all over the country as well as Puerto Rico and the Caribbean.

They were so obviously the best that they were called upon to play not just for the fighting men in their own division, but for soldiers from other divisions, as well as for French troops and French civilians. Later, they played in Paris. The band, which was nicknamed "the Hellfighters," created a sensation. According to Alain Locke in *The Negro and His Music*, published in 1936, "The European musicians could not believe until Jim Europe's musicians played on borrowed instruments that they did not use special instruments quite different from theirs. Such agility, variability of tone, odd intervals, widened tone range were, indeed, a revelation." The French called Europe's music jazz.

After the war ended in 1918, the entire band left the Army and went on a nationwide tour, billing themselves as "65 Musician Veterans of the Champagne and Argonne" (referring to areas of France that had seen action in the war). They recorded for the Pathé Talking Machine and Record Company, and these recordings sold briskly. James Reese Europe was successful beyond even his own greatest dreams. Then, in May 1919, while the band was performing at Mechanic's Hall in Boston, a disgruntled former member of the band, whom Europe had fired, killed him. Europe was only thirty-eight years old.

In his tragically short life, James Reese Europe made a lasting contribution to black music. Not only did he help to organize black musicians for the first time, but he was a tireless defender of black music. He played it, composed it, wrote about it (he wrote many articles about black music that were published in newspapers and magazines), recorded it, and brought it a popularity that most would not have thought possible. When he was killed, he was mourned across the country. The city of New York gave him a public funeral, the first ever for a black man.

Had he lived another few years, James Reese Europe might also have been credited as one of the "fathers of jazz," for it was, after all, the music of his band that was first called by that name. Musicians in New Orleans, however, would have disputed that credit, along with musicians in St. Louis, Memphis, Chicago, and other cities. Jazz had many "fathers," and after World War I the time was right for that particular kind of black music to grow and flourish.

CHAPTER 4

JAZZ

THE SECOND AGE
OF AMERICAN BLACK MUSIC

Jazz grew out of ragtime and the blues. As Alain Locke put it fifty years ago, "The Negro folk idiom in melody and syncopated rhythm gives us 'ragtime,' carried over to harmony and orchestration, it gives us 'jazz.'" Other authorities on black music, including W. C. Handy, saw jazz as a third step on the continuum of black music: spirituals, ragtime and the blues, and jazz.

Just about every authority on music agrees that jazz had begun to develop long before World War I, and that it was cradled in the same areas as ragtime and the blues—in the major towns along the Mississippi. Of these towns, New Orleans was one of the most important in the development of jazz.

New Orleans was a unique city. Because of its history, it had strong Spanish and French influences and a peculiar racial hierarchy that placed the Creoles, who were of mixed blood, somewhere between the whites and the blacks. Before the Civil War, the three racial groups lived together in harmony, and there was much less segregation compared with other southern cities. After the war, however, the population of New Orleans swelled with newly freed blacks, and by 1894, restrictive racial codes were introduced in the city. These codes regarded the Creoles as other blacks, and this did not sit well with the Creoles, many of whom claimed aristocratic French ancestry. For their part, the non-Creole blacks were not too happy having to live side by side with the Creoles. They expressed their resentment in their music by playing as loudly as possible, for the Creoles were fond of soft, delicate music.

Then, in 1897, the city of New Orleans passed another ordinance that restricted all prostitution to an area in the black and Creole section. This had a revolutionary effect on music in New Orleans. Somewhere between fifteen hundred and twenty-two hundred prostitutes set up shop in the area that became known as Storyville, and of course that meant that a large number of saloons and gambling houses sprang up there, too. These "sporting" houses all employed bands, and they brought together black and Creole musicians for the first time. Out of this coming together evolved a standard musical ensemble in which the trumpet or cornet carried the melody and various other instruments—brasses, piano and drums,

57

bass and banjo, or a combination of these—provided the rhythm. This rhythm section was one of the key elements in the development of jazz. In ragtime, the piano provided both rhythm and melody; in jazz, there were more instruments and thus more opportunities for improvising new sounds.

The particular culture of New Orleans provided even more opportunities for improvisation. Storyville brought musicians of many backgrounds together, and there were many occasions at which the bands could play. It was customary in the black neighborhoods for funeral processions to be accompanied by brass bands. And there were two amusement parks where brass bands were the featured form of entertainment. In fact, the black sections of New Orleans were alive with music from morning until night. Once the blacks started trying to drown out the Creoles, the black musicians with the loudest sounds became important in all these circumstances, and it is said that Buddy Bolden had the loudest trumpet in history. It is also said by many that Buddy Bolden was the first man who played jazz.

Buddy Bolden

Not much is known about Buddy Bolden. He was born Charles Bolden in New Orleans in 1868. He was a barber by trade, but when he wasn't pursuing that trade, he was playing his trumpet. He played the blues, but ragtime was his staple, and he played in many places in Storyville, among them Funky Butt Hall (officially Union Son's Hall) and Odd Fellows Hall. He led several brass bands in the 1890s, and they played all

Buddy Bolden (standing, second from left) led several brass bands like this one in the Storyville section of New Orleans in the 1890s. They played at Mardi Gras celebrations, funerals, and various festive occasions. (FRANK DRIGGS COLLECTION)

over. In Storyville, they marched through the streets playing so often that it is said that the prostitutes always recognized the band when it played "Sensation Rag." At funerals, they played a variation of the Baptist hymn "What a Friend We Have in Jesus" on the way to the cemetery and "Oh Didn't He Ramble" on the way back. They played at the Mardi Gras celebrations and on any other occasion that seemed festive. Bunk Johnson, who claimed to have played with Bolden between 1895 and 1899, recalled that there were two amusement parks in New Orleans around that time and that Bolden favored Johnson Park. On arrival with his band, Bolden would stick his trumpet through a hole in the fence and play a call so that people in nearby Lincoln Park would leave and come over to Johnson Park to hear the Buddy Bolden Band.

What distinguished Buddy Bolden as one of the first jazz musicians was his habit of improvising on standard blues and ragtime pieces. Although he could read music, as could one or two of his band members, all preferred to play by ear. In fact, the many black musicians in New Orleans who could not read music considered that a plus for their music, for they believed that their ability to play "with the heart" was infinitely superior to the dulled abilities of music readers. The legendary date of Bolden's first jazz improvisation is 1894, when, in the summer, he and his band improvised a "hot blues" at a dance hall. Many music scholars say, however, that the music generally played by Bolden s band was not real jazz. Still, by about 1900, the music he played—whatever you want to call it—had had a profound effect on other New Orleans musicians, among them the Creoles, who had once been proud of their ability to read and play "legitimate music."

Alan Lomax, author of *Mr. Jelly Roll*, a biography of Jelly Roll Morton, quoted a Creole named Paul Dominguez as saying, "See, us [Creoles], we didn't think so much of this [black] jazz until we couldn't make a living otherwise. . . . If I wanted to make a living I had to be rowdy like the other group. I had to jazz it or rag it or any other damn thing. . . . Bolden cause all that. He cause all these younger Creoles . . . to have a different style altogether from the old heads [who played standard European music as the whites did]."

By the time real jazz began to be identified and talked about, Bolden was in no shape to claim his rightful place in its development. He was a heavy drinker and had syphilis besides, and in 1907 he was committed to a mental institution, where he died in 1931. But there is no question that he profoundly influenced the New Orleans musicians who would merge the two traditions of the Creoles and the non-Creole blacks, among them the towering figure of the early jazz generation, Jelly Roll Morton.

Jelly Roll Morton

Jelly Roll Morton was a Creole who was born Ferdinand La Menthe in New Orleans around 1885. He later changed his name to Morton because he didn't want to be called "Frenchy." His father was a carpenter and sometime trombonist, and Morton began to play musical instruments early in life, among them the harmonica, the drums, the violin, the trombone, and the guitar. As a youth, he played guitar in a three-piece string band and sang with a strolling quartet that specialized in spirituals at funerals and burials. He hung around the big brass bands, carrying the musicians' instrument cases and hoping for a chance to fill in. In addition to getting a lot of musical education that way (he had little formal education), he also learned to play the piano. Pretty soon, he was forced to play music to support himself, for his father vanished, and his mother died when he was fourteen. Morton was fifteen when he got his first job, playing piano in a Storyville brothel. He was seventeen when he composed his first blues, "New Orleans Blues," which became a favorite among the city's bands. Three years later, he composed "King Porter Stomp" and "Jelly Roll Blues." All three of these compositions, and many of his later works, remain jazz classics today.

What made these compositions, and Morton's playing of them, special, was the innovative piano style, which helped bridge the gap between ragtime and jazz piano styles. The ragtime style was marked by strong rhythmic feeling and many notes used mainly as adornment. Morton's style reduced the number of notes played, producing a lighter, more swinging, feeling. That is not to say that his style was simpler. Musicologist Mark C. Gridley explains, "Morton's piano style was quite involved. He often played two or three lines at a time, in the manner of a band. It was as though trumpet parts, clarinet parts, and trombone parts were being heard coming from a piano! Morton's playing featured a variety of themes and much activity within a single piece."

Around 1907, the year that Buddy Bolden was committed to an asylum, twenty-two-year-old Morton left New Orleans and did not settle in one place for any length of time until 1923. He went to Chicago, to Houston, and to California. He returned to New Orleans for a while. Then he took off for the middle South with a seller of patent medicine named Jack the Bear (who sold Coca-Cola laced with salt as a cure for tuberculosis). Morton was in Memphis in 1908 and met W. C. Handy. He was in New York three years later. He toured with several minstrel shows. He spent some time in Los Angeles in partnership with a Creole woman he'd known in New Orleans; they ran hotels and nightclubs, and according to Whitney Balliett, author of *Jelly Roll, Jabbo, and Fats*, "She may have bought him the famous diamond that moved back and forth the rest of his life between pawnshops and one of his front teeth." After that, Morton turned up in Denver and played with the bandleader George Morrison, but that didn't last long either. According to Morrison, "He couldn't stay in one band too long, because he was too eccentric and too temperamental, and he was a one-man band himself. . . . Oh, but he could stomp the blues out. When he got to pattin' that foot, playing the piano and a cigar in his mouth, man, he was gone—he was gone—he was gone!"

Around 1923, Morton went to Chicago, a city he had visited before and soon left, deciding that "nothing was happening." But by 1923, there was a lot happening in Chicago, some of it thanks to the city of New Orleans. In 1917, New Orleans had decided to shut down Storyville. Not only did this action displace a lot of prostitutes; it also displaced a lot of musicians. They made their way to Memphis and Chicago and New York, and it was the infusion of new musical sounds that they brought with them—particularly their habit of group, rather than individual, improvisation—that led to the birth of "real jazz."

Chicagoans claim that jazz did not need any influx of musicians from New Orleans to bring about the birth of jazz in their city. In fact, they claim that jazz was born in Chicago around 1912 and that its "father" was one Jasbo Brown, who played W. C. Handy's "Memphis Blues" and other compositions with great recklessness in a Chicago cabaret. Further, he made his trombone "talk" by putting his derby hat, and later a tin can, at its mouth. The patrons of the cabaret would call out, "More, Jas, more," and so the music came to be called "jazz."

Still, there was a great influx of southern blacks into Chicago between 1910 and 1920—some sixty thousand, increasing the city's black population from about forty thousand to one hundred thousand. These blacks came from all over the South, and it was their very diversity, and the cross-influences between them and the white jazz musicians in Chicago, that helped to create even more exciting jazz and blues sounds in the city.

It was a great time for jazz musicians for another reason: In 1919, the U.S. Congress had passed the Volstead Act, outlawing the sale, manufacture, and transport of alcoholic beverages, and in response more Americans than ever before started drinking and going to private clubs called speakeasies where illegal liquor was sold. Speakeasies sprang up everywhere, and they all needed live entertainment. Jazz seemed to fit in with the illicit atmosphere of these clubs, and jazz musicians got a lot of work. Indeed, there was enough going on in Chicago to cause even the restless Jelly Roll Morton to stay there for five years.

Morton's reputation must have preceded him to Chicago, for almost immediately he began to make records. During his first couple of years in the city, he recorded with cornettist Joe "King" Oliver, also from New Orleans; with the white

New Orleans band the New Orleans Rhythm Kings; and with bands of his own. He also composed a great number of pieces, usually when he needed money, and he could usually count on one of the many sheet music publishers in Chicago to buy them.

Among the keenest purchasers of Morton's compositions were the Melrose brothers. Over the years, they made a lot more money from them than he did; but they are the ones who got him a recording contract with Victor Records and the opportunity to record, with ensembles of his own choosing, the largest body of his own compositions. Between 1926 and 1928, he and various other musicians who worked with him under the name Jelly Roll Morton and His Red Hot Peppers recorded sixteen small-band record sides that remain today classics of early jazz. According to Whitney Balliett, "There is nothing as good anywhere else in Morton's musical life, nor is there anything quite like them anywhere in jazz." Morton wrote them, arranged them, and taught his musicians how to play them. He constantly changed instrumental combinations and emphasized ensemble improvisation, though he did include solos for reed instruments and his own piano. They were wonderful combinations of ragtime, blues, and brass-band music, and these recordings alone assured his place in music history.

That was fortunate for Morton, for by the time he finished making these recordings, jazz developments had suddenly shifted—to New York City and to a different emphasis. While Morton's was basically an ensemble music, an arranger's music, the new emphasis in jazz was on the jazz soloist—on musicians like Louis Armstrong, Coleman Hawkins, Jimmy Harrison,

Jelly Roll Morton's piano style was unique, and at no time was it stronger than in Chicago in the 1920s when he recorded his own compositions for Victor Records. (WIDE WORLD PHOTOS)

Jabbo Smith, and Benny Goodman. That is not to say that Jelly Roll Morton's music lost its audience. Far from it. In New York between 1928 and 1930, when his contract with Victor ran out, he recorded more sides than he had made in five years in Chicago. Among the original compositions that he recorded at that time, quite a few became jazz classics—including "Georgia Swing," "Kansas City Stomp," "Shoe Shiners Drag," "Shreveport Stomp," and "Deep Creek." And many of the young musicians he found in New York to record with him later became jazz greats in their own right.

But in those days, a musician could not make his living from recording. Morton had to hustle jobs. He led bands at Rose Danceland, the Checker Club, and the Lido. He took various hastily assembled bands to play at country clubs in the suburbs. He assembled other bands and played tours throughout the Northeast. He even put together a stage revue called *Speeding Along.* But he could not seem to make the comparatively big money that he thought was his due, being as he was a pioneer of jazz. He watched other jazz musicians, primarily soloists, become more successful than he. He watched newer jazz bands, which played a jazz more acceptable to whites—and which was called classical jazz—get the invitations to play at the big events. He invested what little money he did have in a business venture that failed and, according to legend, became convinced that someone had put a voodoo spell on him. (Voodoo was a very real concept to people who had been born and raised in New Orleans, where there was a strong tradition of belief in the supernatural and in the ability of some people to use the power of the supernatural for their own purposes).

In 1935, Morton moved from New York City to Washington, D.C., where he opened his own small club on the second floor of a building in the city's black district. There, he not only played his songs on the piano, but also tended bar and seated patrons. It was not a great commercial success. Whitney Balliett quotes a photographer named William P. Gottlieb who visited Morton at his little club: "It was a pretty bare place, and I never saw more than a handful of people. Jelly had a big hole in the front tooth where he'd had his diamond, and his face got all crinkled when he smiled. He had a routine he used to go through about how he needed such-and-such a break in order to re-establish himself. He had plenty of bravado, and he exuded optimism. It was a front he never let down."

Three years after his move to Washington, that break happened, though Morton probably did not recognize it at the time. A folklorist named Alan Lomax had not forgotten how important Morton had been to early jazz, and in 1938 he not only interviewed him, but also recorded him playing his original compositions. There was a Jelly Roll Morton revival, and in late 1939 and early 1940 he recorded several sides for the Bluebird label with other jazz greats of his era, including Sidney Bechet, Zutty Singleton, and Sidney de Paris. Not only did Morton play piano on these sides, but he also sang on some of them, and people who know jazz have always wished that he had done more singing on his recordings, for he had a wonderful baritone and marvelous phrasing.

Morton might well have stayed on the East Coast and collected the laurels rightly due "the grand old man of jazz" that he was. But in the fall of 1940, he learned that his godmother had died in California, and worried that some diamonds she had promised him might get into the wrong hands, he headed west. When he got there, he found that the diamonds were gone, but he stayed on. He died in Los Angeles on July 10, 1941, at the age of fifty-six.

Two technological developments in the first three decades of the twentieth century were of immeasurable importance to jazz. The first was the invention of sound recording around the turn of the century. The second was the invention of the radio. The pioneering companies in the area of sound recording were Columbia and Edison and, around 1901, Victor. Popular songs were first recorded in 1909. These early recordings were made on wax cylinders, not on round disks; but the 78-rpm record was soon developed and was used, with improvements, until around 1950.

Without the availability of recordings, it is likely that jazz never would have become as popular as it did. Unlike ragtime, which could be written down and published in millions of copies of sheet music, jazz was so improvisational that it was rarely written down. A jazz musician hardly ever played a piece the same way twice, and if it could not be recorded, it was lost forever, except to those people lucky enough to hear it. The availability of jazz recordings enabled young jazz musicians to study the music of the masters. It also increased the audience for jazz in ways that cannot be measured: Many people who would not have set foot in a roadside inn or brothel or nightclub could listen to jazz on their own record players. What they heard, however, was not very much like the music that was played in clubs or in jazz jam sessions. The music had to be recorded in musical recording studios and was limited to about three minutes. Not until the development of the long-playing record after World War II could a typical jazz performance be recorded.

All kinds of music was recorded, including that of black singers. Blues singer Mamie Smith recorded "That Thing Called Love" and "You Can't Keep a Good Man Down" for Okeh Record Company in 1920. Both songs were the work of a black composer named Perry "Mule" Bradford, and he had written them with the popular white singer, Sophie Tucker, in mind. But he decided that the time had come for black women to start recording, and after a lot of effort he persuaded the white manager of the General Phonograph Company to record Mamie Smith on the Okeh label. While the songs were not really authentic blues, and Mamie Smith's performances of them were not particularly memorable, the record was hugely successful, selling ten thousand copies in its first month, predominantly in the South.

Its success led to the recording of blues and other music by blacks by other record companies. In addition to Mamie Smith and Bessie Smith, also a superb blues singer, many other black female singers began to be recorded. The first black recording company, Pace Phonograph Corporation (later Black Swan Phonograph Company), began operations in 1921. Within a few years, the term "race record" had been coined to describe records aimed primarily at the black market. The segregation practiced in other areas of society carried over to the new technologies.

At the same time that the predominantly male jazz instrumentalists were creating new jazz sounds, dozens of black female singers were creating new blues sounds. The reason black women blues singers were more acceptable to the larger public than black men blues singers is probably the same reason black women performers were more acceptable in the nineteenth century—they were less threatening to whites, and perhaps also to blacks. The blues are very often about love, and whites were not ready to accept a black man singing about love. For that matter, in the black community, it might have been viewed as unseemly for a black man to sing about love on a record, because there was a strong tradition of manliness, which included keeping one's tender feelings to oneself. At any rate, women singers such as Mamie Smith and Bessie Smith were hugely popular in the 1920s, but the woman who became known as "Mother of the Blues" was Ma Rainey.

Ma Rainey

She was born Gertrude Pridgett in Columbus, Georgia, on April 26, 1886, and her singing talent was recognized by the local community quite early. Her first appearance on a stage was in a show at the local opera house when she was about fourteen. Soon she was singing in traveling tent shows, and according to legend, as early as 1902 she had started singing the blues, having first heard that distinctive style in a small town in Missouri.

When she was eighteen, Gertrude Pridgett married a dancer, singer, and comedian some years older than she named Will Rainey, better known as "Pa" Rainey. The two toured with a variety of tent shows, minstrel shows, and circuses for more than a decade. Their act combined music and comedy, and Gertrude was especially popular. On occasion, she toured with shows of her own, performing with groups called The Smarter Set, The Florida Cotton Blossoms, Shufflin' Sam from Alabam', and the Rabbit Foot Minstrels. From 1914 to 1916, she and Pa toured with Tolliver's Circus and Musical Extravaganza and were billed as "Rainey and Rainey, Assassinators of the Blues."

The minstrel shows that she appeared in throughout the South usually followed the harvests, and generally ended up and wintered in New Orleans. There, she met the jazz greats of the city—Joe "King" Oliver, Louis Armstrong, Sidney Bechet, and others. Her friends and audiences in New Orleans thought it stood to reason that if her husband was "Pa" Rainey, then she should be "Ma" Rainey. The nickname seemed to fit. Ma Rainey was a very motherly type—large and not very attractive, but funny and caring and very moralistic when it came to drinking or using bad language in public. By 1915, when she was twenty-nine, according to Sandra Lieb, author of *Mother of the Blues: A Study of Ma Rainey*, she was about ten years older than most of the other performers in the shows and was very maternal toward them. She and Pa never had natural children of their own, but sometime in the mid-teens they adopted a son, Danny, who worked as a dancer in their shows. Several years after that, Ma and Pa Rainey separated and Pa died. Later, Ma married a young man who was not connected with show business, but she retained the name Ma Rainey.

During the late teens, Ma Rainey and Her Georgia Smart Set toured throughout the South with a show that included a variety of acts and usually lasted about two hours. Ma herself

Ma Rainey traveled with various groups throughout the South for nearly thirty years, and her appearance on a stage was always a showstopper. (DUNCAN SCHIEDT COLLECTION)

appeared just before the finale. She made jokes, often about younger men, and then she sang—"Memphis Blues," "Jelly Roll Blues," "I Ain't Got Nobody," and "Walking the Dog." She usually ended with "See, See Rider," a popular song about traveling preachers, and it was a showstopper. Legend has it that she met a fledgling singer named Bessie Smith and helped the younger woman get her first big break in show business. While fans of Bessie Smith dispute that story, the two women did know each other and work together, and Ma Rainey probably had some influence on Smith. Though most people feel that Smith had the better voice, they also agree that Rainey was the better performer.

Ma Rainey may have retired from performing for a while around 1921, but by 1923 she was active again, working with a pianist named Troy Stapp. That year, she also managed to get a recording contract with Paramount Record Company and went to Chicago to make her first recordings. With those recordings, Ma Rainey moved from popular southern singer to a singer of nationwide recognition. "Bad Luck Blues," "Moonshine Blues," and other songs were a balm to the ears of the newly arrived blacks in northern cities. At last they could buy records that featured real down-home music (Mamie Smith, for instance, was a northerner, and so her voice and phrasing were just not the same). Ma Rainey's records also sold well in the South, of course. Paramount booked her on the Theater Owners Booking Association (T.O.B.A.) circuit, the major black entertainment circuit, and she performed throughout the South and the Midwest. She was almost constantly on the road, and for a black entertainer in those days— especially one who was a hard-living forty years old—that was not easy. She had to travel on segregated trains and was denied service in segregated dining cars and in hotels and restaurants in the towns where she played.

By around 1927, Ma Rainey's star was beginning to dim, though she had nothing to do with this change. Developments in the entertainment industry did. Traveling vaudeville shows faced stiff competiton from records and radio. Black communities in the large northern and midwestern cities were turning away from down-home music because it wasn't sophisticated. Just as the Fisk Jubilee Singers had been reluctant to perform the spirituals their parents had sung, so the newly urbanized black populations were now turning away from music that was southern and "countrified." The T.O.B.A. circuit seemed to represent "country" entertainment, and urban blacks stopped going to the theaters that presented T.O.B.A. shows. While Ma Rainey made twenty recordings for Paramount in 1928, she made no more recordings after that.

Ma Rainey continued with the ailing T.O.B.A. circuit until it closed down in June 1930. After that, she toured with her own shows in the South, and despite financial problems, was still rich in talent and audience adoration. When her sister died in 1935, Ma Rainey retired from performing and went home to Columbus, Georgia, to take care of her mother. She acquired two theaters in nearby Rome, Georgia, and operated them until she died of heart disease on December 22, 1939, at the age of fifty-three.

The combination of folk-blues melodies, themes, and images sung by Ma Rainey and other southern black female blues singers came to be called classic blues. It fell from favor for a time, but because it was shared with the larger public through records, it continued to have a strong influence on later singers and on many of the black music styles to come.

*   *   *

After the development of wax cylinders and wax disks for recording, the other important technological innovation was radio, which first became available to the public on a limited scale in 1922. The first radios were crystal sets with earphones, and only one person at a time could listen, but they were soon improved so that many people could listen at one time. Then, in 1926, NBC radio, the first nationwide radio network, went on the air. It is no coincidence that a jazz "explosion" also occurred in the mid-1920s, spewing forth the sounds not only of Ma Rainey and other black female blues singers, but also of jazz instrumentalists, including the man considered by many to be the greatest jazz musician in history, Louis Armstrong.

Louis Armstrong

Armstrong liked to say that he was born in New Orleans on the Fourth of July in 1900, but that date is probably not accurate. More likely, according to his biographer James Lincoln Collier, he was born in 1898. Armstrong's family was extremely poor, and after his parents separated when he was five, he and his mother often went hungry.

Armstrong grew up on the streets. When he was 13, he was arrested and sent to the Colored Waifs Home in New Orleans. This turned out to be a lucky break, for not only was he regularly fed at the home, but also he was taught to play the cornet by the director and the warden, who were amateur musicians. He was released from the home a year later and supported himself by selling coal, delivering milk, and unloading banana boats. He didn't do anything further with his music until 1918, when he was befriended by cornettist Joe "King" Oliver. Oliver had been strongly influenced by Buddy Bolden, and with another musician named Kid Ory, he had formed the most popular band in New Orleans at the time. In 1919, when Oliver left New Orleans for Chicago, he talked Kid Ory into hiring Armstrong as his replacement.

Armstrong played with the Ory band for the next four years until 1922, when Oliver sent for him to join his band in Chicago as second cornettist. It was in Chicago that Armstrong's career really began to flourish: Within two years, he was known as the most powerful, most creative jazz soloist in the city. His private life was also going well; in 1924, he married Lillian Hardin, Oliver's pianist. That same year, he went to New York to join Fletcher Henderson's band and soon was well-known in that city also. It was Henderson who suggested that Armstrong switch from cornet to trumpet, and Armstrong played the trumpet from then on.

Armstrong returned to Chicago in 1925 and organized a recording band for Okeh Records. He'd made recordings in Chicago and New York, but his name had not been prominently featured. With his own band, the Hot Five, his name was predominant, though the others were the best New Orleans–style instrumental soloists around. Their recordings of "Gut Bucket Blues" and "Cornet Chop Suey" are jazz classics, as is "Heebie Jeebies," released in 1926 and the side on which Armstrong introduced his famous scat singing style. Scat singing is the use of the voice like an instrument, substituting nonsense syllables for notes. Armstrong proved as talented at improvising with his voice as with his trumpet, and by 1929 he enjoyed worldwide fame in music circles. His playing style was the standard that others tried to match. Some, like Jabbo Smith, were able to match, and even better, him in technique, but Armstrong's personality and already established fame kept him at the top.

In 1929, Armstrong returned to New York, for he had been invited to star in a black revue on Broadway called *Hot Chocolates*. One of the numbers he played in that show was Fats Waller's "Ain't Misbehavin," and both his live renditions and the recorded version were hugely successful. Now Louis Armstrong was famous outside music circles, too. It was a turning point in his career, for from then on he concentrated not on blues and original instrumentals, but on fronting big bands, playing, singing, and recording popular songs.

Louis Armstrong became one of the most popular entertainers in the world. He toured Europe between 1932 and 1935, and in London received the nickname Satchelmouth, which was later abbreviated to Satchmo (he had a very large mouth, and when he played, his cheeks puffed out to an incredible degree because as a youngster he hadn't been taught by his amateur music teachers the proper way to blow the cornet). Back in the United States, he appeared in the movie *Pennies From Heaven* with Bing Crosby. He fronted more big bands, though by now his famous scat singing was more important than his trumpet playing. In 1947, he formed his own small group, and he continued with that kind of ensemble for the rest of his life.

Armstrong was as popular abroad as he was in his own country, if not more so. Even in the Soviet Union, his name and his music were immediately recognized—and a traveling American was assured of welcome if he or she had brought

By the early 1930s Louis Armstrong was on the verge of international stardom, and not far away from his first European tour, during which Londoners gave him the nickname Satchelmouth (later shortened to Satchmo).

(INSTITUTE OF JAZZ STUDIES, RUTGERS UNIVERSITY)

along some Louis Armstrong records. When he died of a heart attack in 1971, he was mourned around the world.

But in jazz circles, Armstrong was mourned as an individual, not as a jazz artist. Many years before his death, Louis Armstrong had "gone commercial," and music purists could not entirely forgive that. Of course, a good number of them were not alive when Louis Armstrong switched to commercial music, and if they were, they were not trying to make their living at music. Times and tastes changed in the early 1930s, when Armstrong made his switch. It was a strong individual—and one who was either independently wealthy or unconcerned with material things—who managed *not* to "sell out" musically during the Great Depression and the years that followed.

CHAPTER 5

BLACK RENAISSANCE

1920 TO 1940

New York in the 1920s had its own explosion of jazz and black music. It was called the Harlem Renaissance and was due not just to the large influx of blacks, the effects of Prohibition, and the birth of radio, but to several other factors as well. One major factor was the appearance of the first all-black musical on Broadway. *Shuffle Along* was written and produced by two black vaudeville teams, Noble Sissle and Eubie Blake, and Flournoy Miller and Aubrey Lyles, and featured such exciting jazz music and such exuberant jazz dancing that it took New York by storm.

The white music critic Carl Van Vechten decided that if

Shuffle Along on Broadway was so exciting, then a lot more exciting music and dancing must be going on up in Harlem. There, he and other whites discovered not just talented black musicians and singers and dancers, but also talented black writers and poets. The Harlem Renaissance was a literary movement as well as a musical one.

Shuffle Along not only helped to inaugurate the Harlem Renaissance; it also had a strong effect on the musical tastes of Harlemites. Throughout the 1920s, black New Yorkers were more interested in musical revues than in blues singers or the entertainment offerings of the T.O.B.A. circuit. The huge Lafayette Theater, with a seating capacity of two thousand, was the premier Harlem theater. The smaller Lincoln Theater catered to less sophisticated audiences and played many of the blues singers and T.O.B.A. circuit acts.

During the Harlem Renaissance, there were large, whites-only clubs operated by organized crime as outlets for their illegal liquor business. These clubs, like the Cotton Club and Connie's Inn, featured all-black entertainment and favored large musical revues rather than small jazz combos or blues singers, and in the late 1920s their music began to have national influence. The Columbia Broadcasting System started nationwide broadcasts from the Cotton Club, and soon nearly everyone's radio was tuned to the music of Duke Ellington's Cotton Club Orchestra.

Duke Ellington

The music of Duke Ellington epitomizes the sophisticated jazz that grew out of the funkier, down-home variety of New Orleans and Memphis and Chicago. In simple terms, while the music of someone like Louis Armstrong was called hot jazz, Ellington's was cooler; it would come to be called swing. It was a New York–based style, though Duke Ellington was not originally a New Yorker.

Edward Kennedy Ellington was born in Washington, D.C., on April 29, 1899, the son of a White House butler. He showed early promise at the piano as well as at drawing, and his parents encouraged him in both. He had piano lessons as a child, and at Armstrong High School, an all-black trade school, he studied freehand and mechanical drawing. By the time Ellington graduated, he had won a scholarship to Pratt Institute of Fine Arts in Brooklyn, New York. But during high school, he had begun to play piano at various local dances and was earning money at it. He composed music, too—his first piece, "Soda Fountain Rag," was written when he was sixteen. Around that time, his friends gave him the nickname "Duke." Even as a teenager, he fit that name, for he was tall, slim, and good-looking, and always wore a tie and freshly shined shoes.

When Ellington graduated from high school, he had decided to pursue a career in music instead of art. He painted signs by day and played his piano with the small band he assembled at night. To get more jobs, he put an ad in the Washington telephone directory—a larger ad than that of any of the other bands that advertised there—and was soon making enough money to give up sign painting. Ellington and his band members, including drummer Sonny Greer and saxophonist Otto Hardwick, wanted very much to try their luck in New York. When Wilbur Sweatman, a novelty clarinet player, passed through the city and needed musicians for his stage band, Ellington and his group eagerly signed up. They opened at the Lafayette Theater on March 5, 1923.

After they finished their engagement at the Lafayette, Ellington and his band left Sweatman and decided to try to find work on their own in New York. They were unsuccessful, but during their time in the city, they heard most of the major bands and soaked up the sophisticated New York style. When they returned to Washington in defeat, they at least had a better idea of the music that was successful in New York. Not long afterward, they joined Elmer Snowden's Washington Black Sox Orchestra. Snowden, a banjo player, also wanted to get work in New York and finally lined up an engagement in a basement club on West Forty-ninth Street, off Times Square, called the Hollywood Cabaret.

As the Washingtonians, which they thought was a more sophisticated name, they determined to make their mark on the New York music scene. They were successful enough during their first six-month contract at the club that their contract was renewed for another six months. But personal relations among the band members were not so successful. Both Ellington and Snowden were natural leaders, and they disagreed over arrangements and personnel; in February 1924, as the Hollywood Cabaret announced the renewal of the band's contract for yet another six months, Elmer Snowden left to head another band and twenty-four-year-old Duke Ellington became the leader of the Washingtonians.

For the next two years, they played in various New York clubs. They made their first recordings in the fall of 1925 for the Perfect record label—"I'm Going to Hang Around My Sugar" and "Trombone Blues." But they were hardly the talk of the town. They did not have a distinctive sound. As Samuel

Charters and Leonard Kunstadt put it in their book, *Jazz: A History of the New York Scene*, "They were playing exclusively for a white audience and they had managed to pick up all the dated mannerisms of the white Broadway novelty bands."

Then, in the fall of 1926, Ellington hired Irving Mills as his manager. Mills was a savvy white promoter who managed several well-known black bands, including Cab Calloway's, during his career. Though Mills skimmed off more of his clients' profits than he should have, he also gave their careers valuable direction. He suggested that Ellington expand his orchestra and concentrate on the new "jungle style," marked by "growling" horn sounds, that was becoming popular with the black bands. Ellington hired trombonist Joe Nanton, trumpeter Louis Metcalf, and Harry Carney, who played saxophone and clarinet. These men seemed to bring the band to life, and the band's record for Vocalion, "East St. Louis Toodle-Oo," backed by "Birmingham Breakdown," was a great success. Then, in the spring of 1927, the orchestra moved into the Cotton Club.

At the Cotton Club, they were a show orchestra, catering to an audience that favored the slick, commercial style of the Broadway show bands. They were immensely popular, and thanks to the live CBS radio broadcasts, they enjoyed a nationwide audience. They recorded hundreds of sides, including classics like "Black and Tan Fantasy," "Creole Love Call," and "Harlem River Quiver." In fact, they overrecorded. They also lost some of their freshness as they played dazzling, but emotionless, jazz night after night at the Cotton Club. Ellington began to feel less like a bandleader than a master of ceremonies: Finally, in 1931, he and his orchestra left the Cotton Club.

During the 1930s, Duke Ellington and His Orchestra toured in Europe and appeared in several Hollywood movies. Duke added a vocalist, Ivie Anderson, and they crisscrossed the country playing engagements at major theaters and halls. The Great Depression that followed the stock market crash in 1929 seemed to have little effect on Ellington's popularity or success. Recording activity and record sales were hurt, but Duke and his orchestra recorded more than most groups, averaging about nine recordings a year. Two of their biggest hits were Ellington's compositions "Sophisticated Lady" and "Solitude."

Another popular Ellington piece, which he composed in 1932, was "It Don't Mean a Thing If It Ain't Got That Swing." It referred to the new musical sound that his band, and Fletcher Henderson's band even earlier, had popularized. It was a big-band sound that emphasized a blend of arrangement and solo, with reed instrument solos becoming ever more important. Unlike hot jazz, which relied on a great deal of spontaneous improvisation, swing jazz was more carefully arranged, and long practice sessions were necessary for Ellington to teach his band members the sounds he wanted them to make. Swing band musicians were also more likely than hot jazz musicians to have formal musical training and the ability to read music. It was a kind of music that appealed to whites more than hot jazz did, and unfortunately for Ellington and his men, and for other blacks who were playing swing music, white audiences were more comfortable with white musicians playing that music.

There were many white musicians who could play swing, just as they could play hot jazz with the best of the black musicians. Among them was Benny Goodman, born in Chi-

Not only Duke Ellington's music but his personal style as well symbolized the cooler, more sophisticated jazz that arose in New York in the early 1930s. It was a style that appealed to whites, and Ellington became immensely popular. (HASKINS COLLECTION)

cago in 1909 and classically trained on his instrument, the clarinet. He later switched to jazz, and worked with many of the white jazz greats, including Bix Beiderbecke and Jimmy McPartland. Goodman made his first recordings at the age of eighteen with Ben Pollack and His Californians. The following year, 1927, he had his own band. By 1935, he had a big band, which played many Fletcher Henderson arrangements and which was on NBC radio nationwide on Saturday nights. One night while he and the band were on tour, they played at the huge Palomar Ballroom in Los Angeles and were amazed at the crowd's reaction. The people stopped dancing and crowded around the bandstand, and within a few months a swing craze had swept the country. Benny Goodman became known as "the King of Swing." This did not sit too well with the Duke. Other white big bands, including those of Artie Shaw and Tommy Dorsey, were suddenly in demand. Duke Ellington and His Orchestra hardly went hungry, but they did not get the big bookings and the major radio engagements.

It was a discouraging time for Ellington. His mother died in 1935, and his father in 1937. He had been very close to both parents and felt their loss keenly. After several years of touring, he was tired of constantly being on the road, and both he and the members of his band felt that they had lost their musical freshness. In Ellington's opinion, they were bogged down in swing. He told a reporter in the late 1930s, "Swing is stagnant and without a future. . . . Most swing is like the monotonous rhythmic bouncing of a ball. After you hear just so much, you get sick of it because it hasn't enough harmony and there isn't enough of it."

The time had come for a change—a couple of changes, in

fact. In 1939, Ellington broke with his manager, Irving Mills, and took a bigger role in scheduling and promoting his own band. By 1940, he had also hired Billy Strayhorn, a pianist, composer, and arranger who would remain with him for nearly thirty years and never fail, during that time, to stimulate Ellington's musical creativity. Strayhorn wrote the piece that became the orchestra's new theme song, "Take the 'A' Train." Together, Ellington and Strayhorn concentrated on more complex harmonies and more depth in the orchestra's playing. Now, while the solos that were expected of swing music were still included, the rest of the orchestra would play behind the solos, creating a new sound.

Ellington also began to concentrate on arrangements of classical compositions. He and Strayhorn adapted Tchaikovsky's *Nutcracker Suite.* His new agent, William Morris, pointed to the fact that Benny Goodman had already played Carnegie Hall in New York, but that no black band had yet played there; he suggested that Ellington compose a long work for performance in concert at Carnegie Hall. The result was *Black, Brown, and Beige,* which Ellington described as "a tone parallel to the history of the American Negro." There were three sections: The first told the story of slavery, the second emphasized Negro participation in the Civil War and World War I, and the third was about the Negro of the present day (1943). The piece ran almost an hour, and was very controversial because it was a mixture of classical and jazz forms, and neither critics nor audiences were accustomed to such a combination. But Ellington himself was pleased with his effort, and from that time on he devoted as much time as he could to concertpieces. Between 1943 and 1950, he performed an extended concert piece each year at Carnegie Hall, including *Deep South Suite* and *Liberian Suite* (Liberia is a country in western Africa that was founded by free black Americans in the early part of the nineteenth century).

Ellington's ability to change musical styles and his constant musical experimentation were key to his survival as one of the major music makers of the twentieth century. After World War II ended in 1945, the swing era also ended; Benny Goodman's, Tommy Dorsey's, Woody Herman's, and the other major white big bands as well as black bands folded in 1946 and 1947. Duke Ellington's orchestra was feeling the change, too, but Ellington would not disband his group. He wanted to be able to write music and hear it the next day, and he could do that only with a band. They held on, not making much money, but sticking together, and by the mid-1950s were one of the very few big bands still around.

In jazz, the old New Orleans–style performers were back in vogue. There was also a substantial audience for both "bop"— an intense jazz sound—and "cool jazz," a rather fuzzy label that described a style with a relatively small proportion of loud or high notes. Both kinds were performed by small groups in intimate clubs and cabarets. A brand-new sound called rock 'n' roll was developing, too. The Ellington Orchestra didn't have much in common with any of these styles. Fortunately, by keeping his band, though there were a number of personnel changes, Ellington was around to benefit from the renewed interest in the big-band sound that occurred in the late 1950s. By this time, he was the grand old man of jazz, and for the rest of his life he toured both across the nation and abroad, serving as a goodwill ambassador for the U.S.

Department of State on occasion. In the last decade of his life, he embarked on yet another musical form, composing sacred concerts and bringing jazz and folk music into the church. He died in 1974 at the age of seventy-five.

The big-band era, in which Duke Ellington achieved his first popularity, was the one period in American music history when jazz and popular music were one. A primary reason was that people danced to the jazz of the big bands. Another was that the big bands almost always had singers—who put words to the music and, through their good looks and/or personalities, gave people something to identify with. They made jazz less abstract and more enjoyable to people who really did not understand the finer points of improvisation or instrumentation. And yet the greatest of them had voices that were like finely tuned instruments, creating sounds that were as exciting to jazz purists as the most intricate instrumental melodies. When he was writing arrangements for his orchestra, Duke Ellington used to assign a part to female voice as though it were an instrument. Unfortunately, he never had the opportunity to write arrangements for one of the most famous jazz singers of the big-band era—Billie Holiday.

Billie Holiday

Billie Holiday was born Eleanora Fagan on April 7, 1915, in Baltimore, Maryland. Her mother was only thirteen years old at the time, her father only fifteen. They were not married, and so the infant Eleanora was given her mother's last name.

But she knew her father—a trumpet player who called her Bill because she was a tomboy. Eventually, she started to call herself Billie, and eventually, too, she took her father's last name as her own. Unfortunately, her father did not do much for Billie and her mother. Her mother wasn't often around either, so Billie grew up largely on her own. Although little is known about her early childhood, it is clear that she had a number of traumatic experiences, including being raped when she was ten. When the cousin with whom she was living died, Holiday's mother sent for her to join her in New York City.

Life was not much better for her there, although she was happy to be reunited with her mother. The Great Depression came, and they had no money. Holiday was just fifteen years old when she began to sing professionally—she was inexperienced and frightened, but she knew she had to make money somehow. She started at clubs in Queens and Brooklyn, but within four years she was working in Harlem, then considered the black capital of America.

Little is known, too, about Holiday's early musical influences. She thought she recalled hearing Louis Armstrong's recording of "West End Blues" (1928) before she left Baltimore. She probably heard other blues and jazz as a child. Once she started working in nightclubs, she heard many other jazz and blues styles. People compare her singing style with the great blues tradition of Bessie Smith and Ma Rainey, but Holiday herself never mentioned any particular female singers who influenced her. What made people sit up and take notice of her singing was her ability to project the deep sense of loneliness that is essential to the blues.

In 1933, four years after she began singing professionally,

Holiday was singing in a Harlem club called Monette's Supper Club. There, John Hammond heard her for the first time. Hammond was writing a newspaper music column, and he was so taken by Holiday's voice and style that he arranged for her to record. She made her first records in 1933 when she was only eighteen years old, but they did not sell well. Holiday was not particularly concerned. She was far more excited when she got a chance to appear at the Apollo Theater, the most famous theater in Harlem, in April 1935. Ralph Cooper, who was emcee at the Apollo, got her the booking and even bought her an evening gown and slippers. She personally wrote the arrangements for two of the numbers she sang—"Them There Eyes" and "If the Moon Turns Green." The audience at the Apollo was notorious for its toughness, but Holiday brought down the house and was invited back for a week's booking in August.

John Chilton, who wrote a biography of Holiday, described her voice and style this way: "The timbre of her voice was completely individual, and her incredible sense of rhythm and intuitive knowledge of harmony enabled her to phrase songs in a unique way. She could reshape the bleakest melody into something that offered a vast range of emotions to her listeners; her artistry and timing gave her the ability to make poetry out of the most banal lyrics. No one appreciated Billie's talents more than musicians, and many jazzmen (black and white) began to pay regular visits to the clubs where Billie sang."

Among the white musicians who were impressed by Holiday was Benny Goodman, and in the mid-1930s she made a number of records with him. She also recorded with black pianist Teddy Wilson, one of the most innovative pianists of the swing era. During the late 1930s and in the 1940s, Holiday toured with Benny Goodman's Orchestra and also with Artie Shaw's, both predominantly white bands that played popular music. But her uniqueness was that she departed from popular material. Her biggest artistic triumphs were with songs that presented the reality of black life in America, and the reason for the blues—songs like "Strange Fruit," about lynchings in the South, and "God Bless the Child," about personal alienation.

It was that sense of alienation, that deep loneliness no one could share with her, that caused Holiday to become addicted to drugs and alcohol. As a singer, she remained professional, and she toured for a number of years with Count Basie's Orchestra, but eventually her addictions caused her death. She died of lung congestion and other ailments in New York in 1959, at the age of forty-four.

In her comparatively short life, Billie Holiday made a remarkable impression on other female singers. Both Ella Fitzgerald and Sarah Vaughan cite her influence as important to them. Frank Sinatra said in the 1970s that she was "unquestionably the most important influence on American popular singing in the last twenty years." But all the admiration she received, and everything she gave, through her music, were not enough to penetrate the loneliness that made her music so memorable.

While jazz and the blues were the most popular forms of black music, and of music produced by blacks, from the late 1920s to 1940, they did not eclipse other musical forms for

Billie Holiday lived the blues—her ability to convey the reality of black life in America is what made her singing so unique.

(HASKINS COLLECTIONS)

blacks. Black composers, singers, and instrumentalists had continued to pursue other forms, among them classical music and opera. The best of them managed to blend specifically black musical forms with other, traditionally European forms and to create something unique and memorable in the process.

One black composer who first came to prominence in the middle 1930s, William Grant Still, continues to be regarded by many as the greatest black American composer who ever lived. Because his major work was in the area of symphonic music, he was never as well-known as a man like Duke Ellington, most of whose music was more accessible to the larger public. Likewise, Still made very few recordings, and those did not reach the same market as jazz recordings. But in his area, he achieved world renown.

William Grant Still

Still was born in Woodville, Mississippi, in 1895, the son of two teachers. Although his father, who was also a cornettist and leader of a local brass band, died when William was only three months old, the boy grew up surrounded by music. His grandmother sang hymns and spirituals all the time, and his stepfather was an opera buff who listened to recordings of operatic music. As a child, Still took violin lessons. When he enrolled at Wilberforce University in Ohio, however, Still intended to major in science, for his mother wanted him to be a doctor. But he had obvious musical talent, and he soon was directing the college band, writing arrangements for both the band and a string quartet that he organized, and writing his own compositions. He especially enjoyed composing, and while still in college decided that what he really wanted to be was a composer.

In the United States in the teen years of the twentieth century, there were no role models for young William Grant Still—no successful Afro-American composers of music other than jazz or ragtime. But there was such a man in England: Samuel Coleridge-Taylor (1875–1912), son of an African doctor and a British mother, had become famous as a composer of symphonic and operatic music. In the early years of the century, Coleridge-Taylor toured the United States, where he was so enthusiastically received that a Coleridge-Taylor Choral Society was formed in Washington, D.C., specifically to study and perform his music. His composition *Hiawatha's Wedding Feast* was performed by a two-hundred-voice choir and fifty-two musicians from the U.S. Marine Band, and he was a guest of President Theodore Roosevelt at the White House. Sadly for William Grant Still, Coleridge-Taylor had died at the age of thirty-seven and so was not someone whom he could seek out for advice or instruction. Nor did Still have the money to pursue formal musical training, so he left Wilberforce and struck out on his own, determined to get as much musical experience as he could, as well as some money in his pocket. He played violin in dance bands at resorts and for vaudeville shows, and during the summer of 1916 worked for W. C. Handy's music publishing company in Memphis.

On his twenty-first birthday, Still came into a small inheritance that had been left to him by his father. He used that money to enroll at the Oberlin College Conservatory of Music.

His studies there were interrupted by World War I; he enlisted in the Navy and served as a mess (dining room) attendant, the only position available to a black in the Navy at that time. When the white officers discovered Still's musical ability, he was put to work playing the violin in the white officers' mess hall. After the war, he went to New York City but, finding little work, returned to Oberlin. In less than a year, he was back in New York, having been sent for by W. C. Handy to work in Handy's new publishing house. Still also played jazz in Handy's dance orchestra and served as musical director of the Black Swan Phonograph Company. In 1921, he joined the orchestra of the show *Shuffle Along* as oboist.

Also in New York, Still came under the tutelage of Edgard Varèse, a French composer of avant-garde music who had made it known that he wanted to teach a talented black, without fee, to write in the avant-garde style. Still studied with Varèse for two years and developed his skills at composition to a high level. He later won a scholarship to the New England Conservatory of Music, where he studied with George Chadwick, president of the conservatory.

In the mid-1920s, Still began to apply himself to large-scale concert works, and while the early pieces were clearly those of someone searching for his own style and voice, they were nevertheless noticed as the works of a talented composer. It was in the later 1920s that Still began to incorporate black musical influences—spirituals, blues, work songs, jazz—into his compositions. *Levee Land* was published in 1926, as was *From the Black Belt*, a suite for small orchestra; in 1927, Still wrote a ballet with a West Indian setting. In 1930, he wrote a symphony titled *Africa*, but it was his composition *Afro-American Symphony* that brought him his first major success.

The Rochester (New York) Philharmonic Symphony performed it in 1931, the first time in history that a major symphony orchestra had played a symphonic work by a black composer. Four years later, the New York Philharmonic performed the symphony at Carnegie Hall. It remains the most frequently performed of Still's major works, having been presented by hundreds of orchestras both here and abroad, where his work is usually described as characteristically American in its spontaneity and energy.

In 1934, Still received a Guggenheim Fellowship so that he could devote himself to composing full-time, but when the grant, which was renewed twice, finally ran out, he had to turn to other sources of income. As a black, he had no possibility of being resident composer for a large symphony or of counting on commissions to compose major works such as were enjoyed by George Gershwin, the white composer of the music for *Porgy and Bess*. Only because of Still's exceptional talent was he allowed into other areas of music that were generally reserved for whites. He was among the few blacks who managed to get work in radio, and he worked as an arranger and staff composer for both WNBC and WCBS radio; at WNBC, he was the first black composer to conduct a white radio orchestra, though this fact was not well publicized and few in the listening audience were aware of it. In the 1940s, Still worked behind the scenes in Hollywood, where he wrote the musical score for *Pennies From Heaven*, served as music adviser for *Stormy Weather*, which made singer Lena Horne famous, did the orchestrations for *Lost Horizons*, and served as musical adviser or wrote orchestrations for many other films. In the 1960s he wrote music for such TV series as *The Perry Mason Show* and *Gunsmoke*.

William Grant Still was the first black composer to conduct a white radio orchestra and to write musical scores for Hollywood movies. In the 1940s, however, his work in these areas could not be well publicized, because many white radio listeners and moviegoers would have objected. (FRANK DRIGGS COLLECTION)

While such work assured him a good living, Still never forgot his first love, serious composing, and he worked at it whenever he was able. All together, he composed seven operas, four ballets, five symphonies, and a number of works for small instrumental ensembles, piano, and other solo instruments, not to mention choral works and solo songs. His seventh opera, *Highway No. 1, U.S.A.*, had its world premiere in 1963 at the University of Miami. He won numerous awards and fellowships. In many ways, he transcended the barriers of race and yet all the while maintained his integrity as a black man by featuring black American themes.

Still turned seventy-five in 1970, and musical organizations around the country celebrated the event with concerts and festivals devoted to his works. He died eight years later in a nursing home in Los Angeles at the age of eighty-three, one of the few famous and successful black music makers to have lived a long and celebrated life.

The 1930s were William Grant Still's heyday, and the decade was capped off for him in a wonderful way. He was asked to compose music for the 1939 New York World's Fair. Other blacks participated in that fair, among them dancer Bill "Bojangles" Robinson, the star of the hit all-black show on Broadway *The Hot Mikado*. A special shortened version of the show played at the world's fair grounds that summer. But the decade also closed on a somber note for blacks in music, for it was also in 1939 that the black singer Marian Anderson was denied permission to sing at Constitution Hall in the nation's capital.

At the peak of her career, Anderson, who was born in 1902,

was regarded as the world's greatest contralto singer. She was already quite famous in the late 1930s, having made several trips to Europe between 1925 and 1935 and giving a celebrated concert at New York's Town Hall in 1935. But when Anderson tried to give a concert at Constitution Hall in Washington, D.C., she was barred from doing so by the Daughters of the American Revolution because of her race. First Lady Eleanor Roosevelt, wife of President Franklin D. Roosevelt, was appalled, and with others she arranged for Marian Anderson to give an Easter concert on the steps of the Lincoln Memorial. Some seventy-five thousand people heard Anderson sing that day, but it was a comparatively small blow against racism.

In concentrating here on the world of music, it is important that we not lose sight of the larger world in which these music makers lived. It presents a stark contrast. By and large, people involved in the world of music were more interested in music than in skin color; thus it was possible for black female singers to travel with white big bands and for black and white musicians to play together and learn from one another. But in the larger society, racial segregation was as strict as ever. There were places, primarily in the South, where integrated bands could not play. There were places where a black female singer could get up on the stage and sing with a white band, but could not sit on the stage with the band members between numbers. Black singers and musicians could not stay in the same hotels as white singers and musicians, even in New York City; and even in New York City, blacks could not gain admittance to some of the clubs where black musicians and singers were performing. That situation would not change greatly until after World War II, and then only very slowly.

CHAPTER 6

WAR AND REMEMBRANCE

THE 1940s

On December 7, 1941, Japan attacked the United States naval base at Pearl Harbor, Hawaii, and the United States entered World War II, a war that had already been raging in Europe. Immediately, life in the United States changed in a drastic way for nearly everyone, because the energies and the resources of the country were fully committed to the war effort. Men went to war and women went into the factories, food items and gasoline were rationed, and raw materials were directed from other industries to the war industries.

The music business was affected in a variety of ways. Many musicians either enlisted or were drafted into the armed services. Shortages of building materials caused new entertainment-club construction to come to a halt. Shortages of shellac drastically reduced the production of new records, and even big companies such as Victor had to buy up old records and recycle them. Entertainers were asked to do their part for the war effort by performing at war bond sales and for the nation's fighting men at various military bases around the country and abroad.

The heyday of big-band music came to an end, though the bands did not die out altogether. In both jazz and popular music, the small combo became the standard band size. In jazz history, the 1940s are regarded as the beginning of "modern jazz," as distinct from the "classical jazz" that had gone before.

Modern jazz grew out of the swing era, and its major practitioners had played in the big swing bands in the 1930s. The first modern jazz style was called bop, and no one is exactly sure where the term came from. Some people suggest that it came from the vocabulary of nonsense syllables that jazz musicians used in singing jazz phrases—the scat singing that Louis Armstrong first made famous—"do wop de bop," for example. Others suggest that the name of the style derived from the title of a Dizzy Gillespie tune, "Bebop." Gillespie, a trumpeter, was one of the originators of bop. Others were alto saxophonist Charlie Parker and pianist Thelonious Monk. These musicians developed the style independently, but when they came together they inspired one another and worked together to refine the most complex music yet to come out of the black reservoir. Of the three, Charlie Parker is considered by most as the greatest contributor to the development of bop.

Charlie "Yardbird" Parker

Parker was born in Kansas City, Kansas, in 1920, came under the influence of the lively jazz community in that city at an early age, and left school when he was fifteen to make his living playing the alto saxophone. He wandered around the Midwest for about four years and by 1939 had made his way to New York City. He worked when he could in various Harlem clubs before joining the big band of Jay McShann; in 1940, he made his first recordings with McShann. Over the next four years or so, he worked with a variety of bands, including that of Noble Sissle (one of the four creators of *Shuffle Along* back in 1920).

During that time, Parker was developing a style that was considered by some to be revolutionary. Its major characteristic was its tempo, which was breakneck. Even when he played ballads, he tended to ornament slow lines with double-time lines. And even when he was not double-timing, there was a rhythmic undercurrent to his lines that suggested that he was going twice as fast as he actually was. It wasn't just Parker's speed that amazed people; he improvised with great ease and drew from all manner of sources, and he came up with new ways to accent notes that resulted in a high degree of syncopation.

Meanwhile, trumpeter Dizzy Gillespie had been exploring in a similar vein, and when the two came together as coleaders of a combo, bop was born. Their music was faster, their melodies and harmonies more complex, than in classical jazz, and there was less emphasis on arrangements than in swing. Bop was also more aggressive and hard-hitting than swing, and the element of surprise was more important.

To be able to surprise, a jazz musician had to be very skilled on his instrument and very knowledgeable about all kinds of music. The sources on which Parker drew for inspiration were amazing in their variety. Here are some of the influences that musicologist Mark C. Gridley, author of *Jazz Styles*, identifies: "He quoted Lester Young solos [Young was a famous tenor saxophonist eleven years older than Parker]. He quoted traditional melodies such as 'Reuben, Reuben I've Been Thinking' and 'In a Country Garden.' He quoted opera themes such as Bizet's *Carmen*. He quoted twentieth-century European composers' themes, such as Stravinsky's *Petrouchka*. He used melodic fragments and inflections that were traditional in the music of blues singers and early jazz hornmen."

Imagine all those themes and melodies vying with one another in Parker's head! Perhaps he played so fast in order to include as many of them as he could. Perhaps he took drugs in order to quiet them, or to speed them up even more. Many more jazz musicians drank heavily than used drugs, and of those who did use drugs, few were struck down by the habit as young as Charlie Parker. In 1946, he suffered a complete breakdown and spent seven months in Camarillo State Hospital in California. His and Dizzy Gillespie's band did not survive his absence.

When Parker returned to New York, he had gained control of himself and his drug habit, and for the next eight or nine years he was the most influential player in jazz. He played with Erroll Garner's band, Dizzy Gillespie's new big band, and the big bands of Woody Herman (white) and Machito's Latin Band, and recorded with most of these groups. He also led a series of his own groups, using some of the best players

Having licked a serious drug habit, Charlie "Yardbird" Parker enjoyed several years as the premier jazz artist in New York. He is shown here playing with Max Roach and Tommy Potter in a club on West 52nd Street, "Swing Street," in the late 1940s.

(DUNCAN SCHIEDT COLLECTION)

in the bop style, including trumpeter Miles Davis and drummer Max Roach. He wrote a sizeable number of compositions, based on improvisations that he memorized and wrote down, and these were eagerly sought by other bop instrumentalists. Dizzy Gillespie, though himself credited with the development of bop, cited Parker as the primary influence on his own style. Clubs were named after Parker in both New York (Birdland) and Chicago (Birdhouse). His final appearance was at Birdland in 1955. He died that year of a heart attack.

Charlie Parker, though revered among jazz aficionados, never enjoyed the success of a Duke Ellington or a Benny Goodman. The style that he helped to develop was never as popular as swing. Bop recordings never sold in the millions, as a few swing recordings had. Bop performances, demanding as they did a higher level of proficiency, were more serious and less fun to watch. Bop had very few singers, and bop was not considered by the public to be a music to dance to—perhaps it just seemed *too* fast to the average person. And finally, bop and modern jazz seemed so complex that many people felt incapable of understanding it—forgetting, perhaps, that they didn't really have to understand it to enjoy it.

Modern jazz instrumentalists knew that they would not get rich and famous at their music, and they considered those who altered their styles to appeal to the wider public to be "sellouts." That's how many jazz buffs viewed Nat "King" Cole. Yet Cole blazed a trail for black singers that all who came after him were very happy to follow.

* * *

Nat "King" Cole

Though he died in 1965, Cole's voice and the songs he recorded are almost as familiar today as when he was alive. There are few singers in American music history who have equalled his ability to make a romantic song memorable. Yet most people do not realize that Cole began his musical career as a jazz musician and was once considered among the finest in his field.

Cole was born Nathaniel Adams Coles; he dropped the final s in his name when he was a teenager and picked up the nickname King in California when he was playing with his first small combo. Though born in Montgomery, Alabama, in 1919, Cole grew up in Chicago, surrounded by the exciting jazz sounds of the 1920s and 1930s. His most important early influence was the jazz pianist Earl "Fatha" Hines. While still in high school, Cole was forming his own bands, and soon after graduation he joined a touring company of *Shuffle Along*. The show disbanded in California, and for a few years Cole barely managed to support himself by playing piano at beer joints, forming small groups that were unsuccessful, and selling songs he had written for a pittance. His lucky break came when the owner of a Los Angeles club who liked his piano playing asked him to form a quartet. Cole quickly rounded up guitarist Oscar Moore, bassist Wesley Prince, and drummer Lee Young; but on the night of their debut, Young changed his mind about playing in a small combo and failed to show up. The quartet thus became a trio.

During World War II, Wesley Prince was drafted and Johnny Miller took his place. For the next several years, the King

Cole Trio remained together, and after a few lean years, during which Cole was frequently told that his group was an awkward size, it began to achieve considerable success. People who were knowledgeable about jazz recognized that Cole was very important in the transition from swing jazz to modern jazz. He was one of the first pianists to introduce a lighter, more streamlined style of playing. He also perfected a style of accompanying in which chords are played in brief, syncopated bursts, a style that eventually became known as comping.

In 1944, both Cole, as leader of the Trio, and Oscar Moore, as guitarist, were winners in *Metronome* magazine's band poll; they would win that poll and many others in the years to come. Meanwhile, they had made a point of increasing their audience through recordings. They signed a contract with Capitol Records in 1942, and in 1944 had their first hit song, a composition Cole had written back in 1937 called "Straighten Up and Fly Right." Cole sang on that recording, and the group's later records for Capitol also featured his singing, usually ballads.

Ballads had become very popular during the war years, when so many people were separated from their loved ones. It should be noted, however, that the King Cole Trio's records were confined to the "race" market—sold primarily through stores in black communities and played only on black radio stations. The music business was still very segregated, and in 1944 there was considerable white resistance to a black man singing love songs.

Still, the Trio was quite successful. During the 1940s it performed briefly in several Hollywood films. In 1946, it had its own fifteen-minute radio show. Although the time slot, five forty-five P.M. on Saturday, was considered the "graveyard" in radio, the show remained on the air for sixty-eight weeks. This radio show represented a major breakthrough for the group, enabling it to reach the wider white audience more directly than before. The Trio's recordings, with Cole singing, sold better than ever.

In December 1947, Cole went to New York to record some songs in which he was backed not by the Trio but by a string orchestra. Among the songs, recorded almost as an afterthought, was "Nature Boy," written by a barefoot yogi from Brooklyn named Eden Ahbez. It was released as the B side of a song called "Lost April" in March 1948, but it was "Nature Boy" that took the country by storm. The simple message of the song—that the greatest lesson one could learn was to love and be loved—seemed to strike a chord in the hearts of American listeners. Within a week, it was the number-one song in the country, and Nat King Cole became one of the first black male singers to accomplish a nearly complete crossover to the white market. It was a turning point in his career. From that time on, he concentrated more on singing than on playing the piano, and eventually the piano became little more than a stage prop in his performances. His recordings, among them "Ramblin' Rose," "Those Lazy, Hazy, Crazy Days of Summer," "Mona Lisa," and "Unforgettable," consistently topped the white and black record charts for many years.

Jazz critics and jazz fans never forgave Cole for "going commercial," and he found himself constantly on the defensive in explaining why he had turned to singing. There is evidence that he sometimes longed to go back to the piano and jazz,

111

but he was caught up in a life-style that only big money could support. Plagued also by personal problems, he died unhappy and, at age forty-six, tragically early, of lung cancer.

The great popularity of ballads during the years of World War II continued after the war and was a major spur to the young jukebox business. Just about every club, restaurant, and soda fountain had a jukebox by the mid-1940s. The increase in jukeboxes meant a greater demand for records, and the recording business boomed in the 1940s. Ted Fox wrote in his book *Showtime at the Apollo*, "During the 1930s only twenty-six records each sold a million copies or more. Between 1940 and 1945 the figure rose to sixty-eight, and between 1945 and 1950 there were eighty-two. At first, the record companies complained that 75 percent of their output was going to jukeboxes, but as home record players became increasingly popular consumers began buying discs themselves." By the mid-1940s, Americans were buying hit records every week, and for singers especially, having a hit record became all important.

The music business was still highly segregated. Except for Nat King Cole and Billy Eckstine, black singers could hope to see their records only on the "Harlem Hit Parade," not on the white pop charts. But segregated though it was, the black music business was an important enterprise in the black community. As blues and jazz records began to sell more and more copies in the "race" market, it began to occur to producers of black records that there was one major tradition in black music that had not been recorded—gospel music.

Gospel music was an outgrowth of the early slave spirituals. The hymns, sung in church, had all the joy and energy of black worship, for the church was a place where blacks could be themselves and release all their pent-up emotions. Historically, gospel music had been confined to the church, and the most devout blacks considered it a sacrilege to take gospel music out into the secular world, just as they considered popular music, such as the recordings of Bessie Smith and Billie Holiday, to be sacrilegious. But by the 1930s, gospel music had begun to move out of its restrictive, church-only environment. People wanted to listen to gosepl on records, to bring the church and the spirit of its music into their homes.

A pioneer in this effort was Thomas A. Dorsey, known professionally as Georgia Tom, who had played piano for Ma Rainey and had also been a blues singer known for his off-color lyrics until he "got religion." Once converted, he didn't give up his singing career; rather, he decided that the power of gospel ought to be available on records. He took well-known hymns like "Amazing Grace," complete with the exciting "sanctified beat" of a religious revival meeting, and couched them in the sound of the popular music of the day.

By the 1940s, gospel was big business, with dozens of singers and groups recording and touring churches and religious conventions around the country. Rarely, however, did these gospel singers want to perform at the big theaters or clubs where jazz and blues singers and musicians played. Only Sister Rosetta Tharpe found a way to sing at the Apollo Theater in Harlem, for example, and not feel as if she was selling her soul to the devil. Mahalia Jackson, the greatest gospel singer of all time, never played the Apollo, though eventually she, like most other gospel singers, realized that the Lord's music could be sung just about anywhere without harm. Even so, Mahalia Jackson is credited with spreading the message of gospel music throughout the world in a way that no other singer ever has, before or since, and of influencing many divergent musical styles as a result.

Mahalia Jackson

Born in 1911 in New Orleans, as a child Mahalia Jackson had a unique experience of the two separate worlds of black music. On the streets of the city's black section, she heard brass jazz bands and the blues, and in her own home she heard nothing but religious music. Her father, a minister, would allow no other music to be heard in his house, for he was very devout. Jackson recalled in her autobiography, *Movin' On Up*, "In our house we shut everything down from Friday night until Monday. Either you were a Christian and acted like it or you were put out of the church."

Jackson showed at an early age that she had a powerful voice, and she sang in the church choir. Two of her father's cousins were then traveling with "the Mother of the Blues," Ma Rainey, and they wanted to take little Mahalia along with them, but her parents wouldn't hear of it. After her mother died when she was five, Jackson went to live with an aunt, who was just as devout and strict about religion as her father. While secular music was not allowed in the houses where Jackson grew up, she couldn't help but be exposed to it. People were buying windup phonographs and playing Bessie

Smith, Ma Rainey, and Mamie Smith records. She recalled, "You couldn't help but hear blues—all through the thin partitions of the houses—through the open windows—up and down the street in the colored neighborhoods—everybody played it real loud." Jackson heard brass bands at picnics and funerals. She loved all the music she heard. But best of all, she loved the songs that were sung in the church next door—the Sanctified Church. She was a Baptist and liked the "sweet" songs her congregation sang, but there was nothing like the singing of the Sanctified Church congregation: "Those people had no choir and no organ. They used the drum, the cymbal, the tambourine, and the steel triangle. Everybody in there sang and they clapped and stomped their feet and sang with their whole bodies. They had a beat, a powerful beat, a rhythm we held on to from slavery days, and their music was so strong and expressive it used to bring the tears to my eyes."

Mahalia Jackson finished eighth grade at a nearby school, then hired herself out as a laundress working ten hours a day. She had no intention of remaining in New Orleans, and the more she heard about the North from relatives who had moved there, the more she longed to go and see for herself. When she was sixteen, having saved enough money from doing laundry, she went to Chicago with an aunt.

When Jackson arrived in Chicago in 1928, that city's South Side was the second-largest black community in the country after Harlem. The majority of blacks there were recent arrivals from the South, and they had established churches, which remained the center of their lives just as in the South. Jackson joined the Greater Salem Baptist Church, which became her "second home." She sang in the choir and went to the church socials and picnics. With others in the choir, she formed a singing group called the Johnson Gospel Singers, which sang all over the South Side. Of the group members, Jackson was the most serious about gospel singing, and eventually she began to sing by herself. By the middle of the Depression years, she was singing in small black churches from New York to California, though in order to support herself she still had to do laundry for Chicago's North Side white families in between.

At some point during her travels, Jackson met Thomas A. Dorsey, whom she called Professor A. Dorsey, and the two began performing together on occasion. Probably with his help, she made her first recording, "God Gonna Separate the Wheat from the Tares," in 1934, but it was not particularly successful. She married in 1935, and her husband, Ike, along with many others, urged her to sing secular music; but she refused to do so. Instead, she saved her money and opened Mahalia's Beauty Salon and Mahalia's House of Flowers. These successful businesses supported her while she pursued her love of gospel music. She continued to make records, but it was not until 1946 that she had a hit. Decca recorded her rendition of "I Will Move On Up a Little Higher" that year; the record sold nearly two million copies.

The people who bought the record were mostly blacks, but a white professor of music at the New School for Social Research in New York City named Marshall Stearns heard it and invited Jackson to sing at a music symposium near Tanglewood in Massachusetts. The music teachers at the symposium were struck by the range and control Jackson had over her rich contralto voice. They tried to analyze the meter and insisted that she was singing twelve-twelve time, while she was just as insistent that she sang in four-four time.

At any rate, Jackson's life was never the same after that. She said it was as if a dam had broken. The music professors spread the word, and she was invited to sing at concerts, at the National Baptist Convention, even on Ed Sullivan's TV show. In 1950, she made her debut at Carnegie Hall. Two years later, she made her first tour in Europe, and two years after that, she had her own local radio program on CBS in Chicago, which became her own TV program a year later. The TV show was so successful in Chicago that she inquired about making it a network program. At that point, the "dam" that had "broken" several years earlier quickly reassembled itself. Jackson was informed by the producers that the program's sponsors would never allow it, for fear that southern audiences would boycott their products.

Mahalia Jackson was no stranger to segregation, but it never ceased to gall her that people who called themselves Christians would act the way they did toward blacks. She was not the only successful black performer who ran up against a stony wall of segregation in the South—Nat King Cole was attacked on a stage in Birmingham, Alabama, by members of a local White Citizens Council. Unlike Cole, who chose not to publicly fight against segregation, Mahalia Jackson became active in the civil rights movement that began in the late 1950s with the Montgomery, Alabama, bus boycott and the work of Martin Luther King, Jr. In 1963, she sang on the steps of the Lincoln Memorial before the tens of thousands of people who had assembled for the March on Washington for Jobs and Freedom.

Mahalia Jackson was active in the movement for black civil rights that began in the late 1950s. In 1960 she not only honored W. C. Handy, "Father of the Blues," when a statue of him was dedicated in his hometown of St. Louis, Missouri, but by choosing to sing Handy's composition "I'll Never Turn Back," she also sent a message that black people were not going to give up their fight for civil rights. (WIDE WORLD PHOTOS)

Jackson died in 1972, having brought traditional gospel music to audiences around the world and having influenced countless female singers. She also died knowing that she had never disgraced her parents' memory by taking gospel into nightclubs or putting out a "pop gospel" record, both of which she considered "blaspheming against the Holy Ghost." "I make two kinds of gospel records—one for Negroes who like to tap their feet, and one for those who like religious songs sung for them," she said in her autobiography. "But I would never sing a song to be laughed at or to help sell a bottle of whiskey!"

For black music, the 1940s were years of transition. They saw the development of modern jazz from swing. They saw the popularization of singers, due to the public interest in ballads and the burgeoning record industry. They saw the first successful crossovers into the white music world by a few blacks like Nat King Cole. In the next decade, these developments would continue, and flower.

CHAPTER 7

RHYTHM, BLUES, AND ARIAS

THE 1950s

In 1949 *Billboard* magazine stopped calling black hits "race records." It inaugurated a new category on its chart: rhythm and blues. Although this did little to change the segregation of the music world, it did signal a different attitude toward black music, allowing it a toehold in the mainstream. Quoted in *Showtime at the Apollo*, singer Ruth Brown defined the music from a singer's point of view: "We were working under all kinds of adverse situations . . . consequently, there was a lot of hurt that went along with it. What really sustained us was the music. All of the things that went wrong during the travels, or the harassment, you took that out onstage. You got up and started to sing, and I think that's where the feeling for the lyric comes from. It was a total experience. The rhythm covered up for the blues. That's my estimation of what rhythm and blues was. The rhythm, the beat, covered up the blues, but the blues were inside." Dinah Washington, an important blues singer of the period, earned the title "Queen of the Blues" because, as Charles Davis, a former member of her band put it, "How many other singers could make a whole band cry?"

Black Americans had plenty to be blue about in the years after World War II. Though blacks had fought in large numbers and had distinguished themselves in "the war to make the world safe for democracy," they found that at home they did not enjoy the freedoms that they had fought to ensure for people abroad. They were still second-class citizens in the North and little more than slaves in the South. They were angry, but felt powerless to do anything about their situation. So they expressed their feelings in their music.

Any number of black singers and musicians were placed in the rhythm and blues category—if only because that was the only place to put most blacks in the music business—but those who are considered pioneers in the area were almost exclusively from the South. They were not widely popular outside the South and did not enjoy a following among northern urban or middle-class southern blacks, for both groups still regarded the blues as "country" music. As Isaac Hayes told Gerri Hirshey, author of *Nowhere to Run*, "As a kid in the fifties I was taught to be *ashamed* of the blues. We thought it was plantation darky stuff. And that was miles from where *we* wanted to be." But once people like Chuck Berry and Bo Diddley started putting their blues to a driving, rhythmic beat, few in their audiences could resist being caught up in it.

Bo Diddley

Bo Diddley was born Ellas Bates near McComb, Mississippi, in 1928. His father died soon afterward, and the rest of the family was taken in by the McDaniels, whose name Ellas took. When he was six, the family moved to Chicago, and Ellas attended grammer school there. A loner and a fighter, he received the nickname Bo Diddley from schoolmates who had heard of a "mean sapsucker" slave by that name in southern folklore. Although Chicago was alive with jazz, Diddley's mother wanted her son to have no part of it, and for seven years he studied classical violin with the music director of the local Ebenezer Baptist Church.

Diddley was classified as "slow" in school, and on completion of junior high he was enrolled in a vocational high school. He was more interested in music than in learning a trade, however, and over his mother's objections preferred the guitar and harmonica to the violin. With a friend named Jerome Green, who played the maracas, he entertained on street corners for quarters. Eventually, he quit school altogether and formed a group called the Langley Avenue Jive Cats, which got bookings on weekends at the local 708 Club. On weekday nights, he and Green continued to perform on street corners, and developed a popular routine based on a ghetto street-corner pastime, the dozens—trading outrageous but good-humored insults.

When World War II broke out, both Diddley and Green were drafted into the Army. On being discharged, they teamed up again, working clubs whenever they could and still working the street corners. They were often forced to do other things in order to make a living, and Diddley sometimes worked as a semiprofessional boxer. When he had enough money, he bought himself an electric guitar, and with it he was able to create a driving, pounding bass line. He treated the guitar almost like a person and developed a sexually suggestive way of moving with it. He and Green had a distinctive, syncopated beat and an exciting way of delivering lyrics that was basically rap and nonsense.

By 1955, postwar prosperity had found its way to the record business. The 45-rpm disk was taking over from the old 78-rpm record, and since it was lighter, more durable, and easy to make and distribute, it gave a real boost to record companies. More and more people were buying records and record players; every club worthy of the name had a jukebox. There were more record companies that, along with the already established ones, were signing up new talent. There was a greater interest on the part of whites in black music. In Chicago, the Chess Record Company already had contracts with bluesmen Muddy Waters, Howlin' Wolf, and a crazy guitar player named Chuck Berry, and was actively seeking more.

Diddley's small-time agent had managed to sign him to a contract with Aristocrat records, but Diddley had heard that Chess was the label to go with and signed with them. "I found out that I was on two different contracts," he recalls, "and I didn't know what the hell I was signing anyway." Chess issued his first record, "Bo Diddley"/"I'm a Man," on May 15, 1955, and both sides became immediate rhythm and blues hits. What was distinctive about them was neither the melody nor the lyrics, but the incredible, all-important beat. Diddley's "basic bottom" beat was soon being widely imitated, but he says resignedly, "You can't copyright a beat." Shortly after the release of Diddley's first record, Chess issued Chuck Berry's "Maybellene." In a short time, Diddley and Berry were the stars of the Chess label, although Berry had more hits. In fact, the twenty-four-year-old Berry captured the *Billboard* triple award that year for "Maybellene"—biggest rhythm and blues record, biggest rhythm and blues record on the radio stations, and most-played rhythm and blues record on juke-boxes.

Diddley was in demand all over. His performances at the Apollo Theater in New York that fall became part of Apollo legend. Dressed in black, wearing a black Stetson hat, and playing a rectangular guitar that he had designed himself and had custom-made, he whipped the audience into a frenzy with his driving beat and his wild gyrations. He swiveled his hips, played the guitar's strings with his teeth, played it behind his back—and the audience went wild. When Diddley appeared on Ed Sullivan's *Toast of the Town* TV show, the cameras stopped showing him from the waist down after about one minute, for his hip gyrations were deemed improper for TV audiences to see.

A couple of years earlier, Alan Freed, a white disc jockey, had broken radio's unwritten color line by playing rhythm and blues records on a white radio station in Cleveland. He then moved to New York and did the same thing. Freed is credited with originating the term rock 'n' roll—to describe the distinctive sound of Bo Diddley. "I was the first son of a gun to get called rock 'n' roll because they didn't know what the heck to call it," Bo says. "I had that funny-soundin' guitar and they just did not know what to say. Alan Freed had that radio show and I was on and he said, 'Well, here's a man gone rock 'n' roll you right outa yer seat.' I was the one that started the whole thing."

Freed started organizing large rhythm and blues and rock 'n' roll road shows, and Bo Diddley traveled with many of them during the 1950s. Diddley also played the major theaters, white and black, in big cities across the country. Often he was billed with jazz acts, for his music was so unique it was hard to classify and was frequently referred to as jazz. Actually, this benefited him, for jazz was far more acceptable to the general population than rhythm and blues or rock 'n' roll, both of which were still regarded as almost exclusively black domains. Not only was he popular in the United States, but by 1956 his records were being released in England and he was performing in Australia.

Bo Diddley was soon being widely imitated. When a young kid from the country named Elvis Presley made his first trip to New York, he went straight to the Apollo Theater and there saw Bo Diddley drive the audience crazy. On his first TV appearance, on the *Tommy and Jimmy Dorsey Show,* Elvis made headlines with his gyrating-hips performance. Muddy Waters, who had influenced Bo Diddley before he was successful, now was clearly influenced by Bo Diddley—he made "I'm a Man" his theme song. A young, white Texan named Buddy Holly was incorporating Diddley's double-rhythm guitar pattern into his own playing.

By the late 1950s, whites had moved into rock 'n' roll in such numbers that black performers such as Bo Diddley and Chuck Berry were practically eclipsed. The rawness of Diddley's early hits now seemed too rough edged for the more refined (some would say less earthy) rock 'n' roll tastes of the last years of the decade. His recordings of the late 1950s were not hits. Diddley suffered also because his songs had never been played on radio as much as those of other performers. They were hard to categorize and difficult to fit into most record stations' playlists. He had relied primarily on TV and live performances to reach his audience. But without radio play, he could not get his records widely heard.

Diddley had married by this time, and when he realized he was not making enough money to support a family, he took a job as a sheriff in a small town in Ohio, continuing to write music and to perform on occasion. In late 1959, he broke onto the charts again with "I'm Sorry"/"Crackin' Up," both in a more refined style. He followed that success with "Say Man," which was in the Top 40 on the U.S. Hot 100 chart for several months. "Say Man" was vintage Diddley and Green fooling around and playing the dozens—Diddley saying that Green's girl was the ugliest chick he'd ever seen and Green coming right back at him. There is a line about how a girl has to sneak up on a glass just to get a drink of water. The two didn't even know they were being recorded. With some clever instrumental dubbing, it became a big hit.

In the early 1960s, Diddley had a couple more hits and cut several albums that sold respectably well. He was able to perform steadily thanks to renewed interest in early rock 'n' roll. By the middle of the 1970s, the fact that rock 'n' roll was twenty years old brought a new wave of interest in the pioneers of the form, and Diddley appeared on *Dick Clark's Good Old Days* TV special, on the *Donnie and Marie Show*, and on other TV shows. Although he had continued to write songs and to do occasional new recordings, 1970s audiences seemed to want him to do only his early classics, and he obliged.

Since 1979, Diddley has toured often with individuals and groups, including The Clash and Bruce Springsteen, who cite him as one of their most important early musical influences. Others who point to the influence of Bo Diddley are the Rolling Stones and the Grateful Dead. Bo Diddley lives in Hawthorne, Florida, when he isn't on tour.

It has been noted that jazz was far more acceptable to the general population in the 1950s than was either rhythm and blues or rock 'n' roll. Partly that was because of the lingering success of the big-band sound. Though by the 1950s there were not many big bands left, big-band jazz, however commercialized, had educated the general public to the sounds of jazz that were now being played by small combos. In colleges across the country, jazz was the favorite music—the white jazz musician Dave Brubeck cut an album called *Jazz Goes to College*, and most self-respecting collegians regarded it as an important item in their campus-bound baggage. Nat King Cole's trio was winning *Billboard* college polls as best small combo. The 1950s were a ripe time for jazz and for new developments in jazz. During that decade, many changes occurred in jazz. There was a transition from bop to "cool" and "West Coast" jazz, a transition from bop to "hard bop," and a transition from "cool" and "West Coast" and "hard bop" to "modal jazz"and "free jazz." One single jazzman was important in all of these transitions—Miles Davis.

Miles Davis

Davis was born Miles Dewey Davis, Jr., in 1926, in East St. Louis, Illinois, the son of well-to-do parents who could afford to encourage his early musical talent with music lessons. During the early 1940s, many important jazz musicians passed through St. Louis, just across the Mississippi from East St. Louis, and the teenage Davis was already expert enough on the trumpet to sit in with such jazz greats as Charlie Parker and Coleman Hawkins when they came to town with the Billy Eckstine band. On graduation from high school, he enrolled at the prestigious Juilliard School of Music in New York City.

Davis attended classes by day. At night, he had ample opportunity to practice what he was learning on West Fifty-second Street, a long strip of jazz clubs of world renown. There, he again had the opportunity to sit in with Coleman Hawkins and Charlie Parker, as well as with Benny Carter and a host of others. Soon, he was touring with Carter, with Billy Eckstine, and with Charlie Parker.

In 1949, Davis formed his own interracial band, which included Lee Konitz on alto sax, Gerry Mulligan on baritone sax, and Max Roach on drums. All were superb musicians, and one of Davis's strengths throughout his long career has been his ability to select exceptionally talented sidemen. What made their sound different was that neither tenor saxophone nor guitar was used—the instrumentation was filled out by

French horn, tuba, trombone, and a rhythm section. What also made their sound different was the subdued feeling they brought to their solos, and the overall delicate, "cool" effect. This band was not loud or brassy. The recordings they made on Capitol Records became known as "The Birth of the Cool," and these recordings are cited as the first to exemplify the innovation of cool in jazz.

Cool jazz is generally defined as quiet jazz, with very few loud or high notes. It was a sound that both Davis and Konitz had been experimenting with individually, and that pianist Lennie Tristano, pianist-composer Gil Evans, and pianist-composer-arranger-bandleader Claude Thornhill had been developing as well. Davis and his band consolidated these influences. But there is one element of cool jazz with which many people credit Davis alone, and that is his skillful use of silence. During his solos, he would often allow several beats to pass without playing—the listener would hear only the bass and drums. It was an exceptionally dramatic technique.

The cool sound had a great effect on West Coast jazzmen, and by the middle 1950s, there was an identifiable "West Coast style." The West Coast jazzmen were mostly white— Dave Brubeck was the most influential pianist in this style— but when it came to trumpet playing, the white trumpeters were heavily influenced by Miles Davis. The style was characterized by light, cool, melodically simple improvisation— some people called it polite jazz. By the time jazz critics and fans had defined and named it, Miles Davis had gone on to other things. In fact, he had taken up a style that was almost the direct opposite of the West Coast style. It was called hard bop.

Davis's nine-piece group (called a nonet) had been widely

praised by musicians, but had not done very well commercially. Eventually, he disbanded that group and formed a quintet, which included Red Garland on piano, Paul Chambers on bass, Philly Joe Jones on drums, and John Coltrane on sax, as well as Davis himself on trumpet. Once again, he had chosen superbly talented musicians, and their recordings for Prestige Records in 1955 and 1956, and for Columbia Records in 1956, are regarded as classics. Alto saxophonist Cannonball Adderley joined the group and helped it render more classic recordings in 1958. The hard bop sound the group played had evolved smoothly from the bebop of the 1940s— it was earthy and funky, and its harmonies were derived from gospel music. It was not as popular as West Coast jazz, though it lasted longer.

By the late 1950s, Miles Davis was back to the delicate techniques he had employed a decade earlier. He now had a highly personal sound, which he created by using a Harmon mute without its shank, or stem. He favored more down-tempo pieces, and his 1959 recording *Kind of Blue* is often cited as an early example of "modal" or "free" jazz. He was among the first musicians to make recordings using the fluegelhorn, a three-valve horn with a sweet sound, and was credited as the musician most responsible for its later popularity (it is Chuck Mangione's instrument).

In the meantime, Davis had been going through some personal changes, including a serious addiction to heroin (which he conquered after a four-year struggle) and a change of attitude about being black in a racist society. In 1959, while he and his group were playing at Birdland, in New York City, Davis had been beaten by a policeman as he took a breather outside between sets. After that, his political stance became more and more militant. Musically, the 1960s were a time of regrouping for him. Feeling bereft of ideas, he did what he had done before—surrounded himself with young, talented musicians and allowed their ideas to affect his own music. The Miles Davis Quintet of 1964–68 experimented with rock and funk and is credited with major influence in the fusion of jazz and rock. For his own part, Davis was experimenting with the higher registers of his trumpet. After recording *In a Silent Way* and *Bitches Brew,* both of which were released in 1969, several of Davis's sidemen formed important jazz-rock groups: Herbie Hancock's Head Hunters, Chick Corea's Return to Forever, and Wayne Shorter's Weather Report. In the early 1970s, Davis's groups were distinguished by the use of several keyboards; in the mid-1970s, his rhythm sections sometimes included two or three guitars.

Around 1975, Miles Davis experienced another period of personal crisis, due primarily to illness. He dropped out of public view completely, neither recording nor touring. During this time he met the actress Cicely Tyson, who is credited with helping him through this difficult period. They were married in 1981, and that same year Davis reemerged as a musician and bandleader. This time, his group included an electric bass and guitars. Some critics complained that he had surrounded himself with electronics and relied too much on gadgetry, that his trumpet playing was undistinguished. But then, he had not played the trumpet in some time, and it is a very taxing instrument. By 1984, his trumpet was strong again, piercing through the electronic environment; his album released that year, *Decoy,* was voted jazz album of the year in a *Down Beat* readers' poll.

Miles Davis has been innovative for so long that many of

One of the most innovative jazz musicians who ever lived, Miles Davis has had a career marked by abrupt musical and personal changes. This photograph was taken in the early 1970s, not long before he dropped out of sight—neither recording nor touring—for nearly ten years. (DUNCAN SCHIEDT COLLECTION)

today's fans are not familiar with all the different phases of his career. Many jazz fans do not understand why Davis is considered a legend, for they point out that he is not as skillful a trumpeter as Dizzy Gillespie, for example. But what distinguishes Miles Davis is his tremendous skill as an improviser and his equal skill as a composer, arranger, and bandleader. He has never lost the ability to surround himself with extraordinary musicians who inspire him and each other. Mark C. Gridley wrote: "A large portion of modern jazz history is documented in Davis-led recording sessions. . . . Davis was not personally responsible for all the ideas at these recording sessions, but he was the overseer, and much in the progression of modern jazz styles has occurred within Davis-led groups."

So far, this chapter has focused on specifically black musical forms—both rhythm and blues and jazz originated among blacks and were later adopted by whites. But while some blacks were developing and sharing unique black musical forms, other blacks were distinguishing themselves in musical forms that were traditionally white. While they did not break musical ground, they broke social ground, paving the way for greater acceptance of blacks and their music. The 1950s saw major progress for blacks in the world of opera.

More Than Otello and Aïda

Opera is a form of musical drama in which a story is acted and sung by singers in costume, with scenery and orchestral accompaniment. It has existed for many centuries in many cultures (it existed in ancient China, for example), but opera as we know it originated in Italy in the sixteenth century and then spread to Germany, France, England, and other European countries. Probably the most famous composer of operas that are performed today was Giuseppe Verdi (1817–1901); other than Italians, Germans probably composed more operas that are popular today than composers from any other country. Because most composers of operas were white Europeans, the majority of traditional operas feature white characters. But there are exceptions. The opera *Otello* is based on the play *Othello: The Moor of Venice* by Shakespeare about a noble Moor who kills his white wife in a fit of jealousy. The opera *Aïda* is about an Ethiopian princess serving as a slave in Egypt. The opera *Madame Butterfly* is about a Japanese woman. When these operas were first presented, they had all-white casts, and this held true for some time.

Opera was introduced in America in the 1800s, a century later than plays had been introduced because operas were comparatively expensive to stage—what with the scenery, costumes, and orchestra, not to mention the starring singers. By the 1870s, a small number of free blacks had been exposed to opera, and liked it; they formed the Colored American Opera Company, which gave performances in Philadelphia and Washington, D.C. As we have noted, ragtime composer Scott Joplin composed a folk opera, *Treemonisha*, in 1911, though it was not given a full production until the 1970s. When Joplin was alive, and for many years after that, the majority white society considered opera a white musical form and could not imagine blacks in it—even in nonwhite roles like Othello and Aïda.

Caterina Jarboro was the first black woman to appear in a

leading role with an American opera company: She played the title role in the Chicago Civic Opera's performance of *Aïda* at the Hippodrome Theater in New York in 1933. She was not, however, a regular artist with the company. Her appearance did not signal any new trend. Not until 1945 did a black achieve the status of regular artist with a company; in that year, Todd Duncan made his debut as Tonio with the New York City Opera in *I Pagliacci*. Not long afterward, soprano Camilla Williams became the first black to sing the title role in *Madame Butterfly*. Though these were still isolated incidents, they would eventually prove to be pioneering efforts in establishing a black presence on the American opera stage. The real breakthroughs occurred about ten years later, in the 1950s.

The operas didn't change in those ten years, but the sensibilities of opera producers did, and opera lovers apparently went along with the change. It is risky to make pronouncements about a whole group of people, even if it is a small group, but we can suggest that people who truly value talent are less likely to be sidetracked by matters of race or gender. There has almost always been less of a color barrier in the world of entertainment than in the world at large, for example. And it was in the world of entertainment that black Americans were first accepted as equals.

In the United States, the Metropolitan Opera is the premier opera company. A black appeared for the first time on its stage in 1955. Black female singer Sissieretta Jones ("the Black Patti") was supposed to have performed there in 1892, and actually had a contract; but a fire closed the house down soon after, and her debut never took place. More than sixty years later, none other than Marian Anderson, who had become so famous in 1939 when the Daughters of the American Revolution would not allow her to perform at Constitution Hall in Washington, D.C., became the first black to sing at the Met. She played the role of Ulrica in the opera *A Masked Ball. Variety*, the entertainment newspaper, noted that it was fitting that Marian Anderson should have been the first black to sing at the Met: "Like Joshua, but more quietly, [she] had fought the battle of Jericho and at last the walls came tumbling down." Three weeks later, baritone Robert McFerrin, the first black male to join the company, made his debut at the Met, playing Amonasro in *Aïda*. The following year, soprano Mattiwilda Dobbs, who had already become famous in Europe, made her debut as Gilda in *Rigoletto*.

The most famous black American opera singer in history came to public notice in the 1950s. The voice of Leontyne Price has been called "the voice of the century." Price was a nine-year-old in Laurel, Mississippi, when she decided to become a singer. Her mother took her to a concert at the Jackson, Mississippi, Civic Center: "We sat way, way up in the rafters," recalls Price, "and I saw this fantastic lady come out onstage in a white satin gown. She had a fabulously regal bearing. It was Marian Anderson, and I just said to myself, 'I don't know what she's doing, but I sure want to do some of that one of these days.' "

After graduating from Central State College in Wilberforce, Ohio, Price, who was born February 10, 1927, attended the Juilliard School of Music in New York on scholarship. While at Juilliard, she sang in a student production of Verdi's *Falstaff*. Virgil Thomson, the noted composer and critic, heard Price and selected her to sing in the revival of his opera *Four*

Saints in Three Acts. She made her Paris debut in 1952 at the International Arts Festival. The following year, she sang the part of Bess in *Porgy and Bess* in Vienna. She made her New York debut at Town Hall in 1954, her Los Angeles debut in 1955, and debuts with the San Francisco Opera Company in 1957, the Vienna State Opera in 1958, and the famous La Scala Opera House in Milan, Italy, in 1960. All these performances at the great opera houses of the world were carefully planned to lead up to Price's ultimate goal—the Metropolitan. She made her debut there in January, 1961, in *Il Trovatore.* That fall, she sang the title role in *The Girl of the Golden West.* She would return to the stage of the Metropolitan many times, but probably her most triumphant performance was in 1976, when she sang the title role in *Aïda.* She had first sung the part back in 1957 with the San Francisco Opera and had since sung it on many stages. To opera lovers, Price had the perfect Verdi voice, and in her career she has probably sung more operas by Giuseppe Verdi than by any other composer. But she was especially compelling as Aïda. Even Italian critics wrote, "Our Verdi would have found her the ideal Aïda."

By 1984, Leontyne Price was in semiretirement, singing primarily at charity benefits and resting on her laurels as "the voice of the century." Her appearances on such TV programs as *The Tonight Show* and her many records helped to make opera more popular, and she has helped pave the way for other talented black female opera singers, including mezzo-sopranos Grace Bumbry and Barbara Conrad and soprano Jessye Norman. Blacks in opera are still a comparative rarity, however, and this is especially true of black male opera singers. While there have been many fine male singers, including

Leontyne Price takes a curtain call after her final performance as Aïda in early 1984. Critics agreed that this role in the opera by Giuseppe Verdi was her greatest.   (WIDE WORLD PHOTOS)

McHenry Boatwright, William Warfield, George Shirley, Simon Estes, and Arthur Thompson, there are still far more female than male opera singers. "Why are there so few black males in my particular creative art form?" Leontyne Price once asked. "You can't tell me there isn't a wealth of black male talent. A black hero is a greater threat, socially, than a black heroine." The first time the Metropolitan Opera presented *Porgy and Bess* with an all-black cast was 1985. Still, the 1950s were a time when blacks in opera enjoyed unprecedented opportunities, and though progress has been slow, the opera world has never gone back to its pre-1950s ways.

There was black progress in many areas in the 1950s. In 1954, the U.S. Supreme Court ruled that "separate but equal" education was unconstitutional, and thus outlawed segregated schools. Toward the end of the decade, southern blacks began to seek an end to other types of segregation. Blacks in Montgomery, Alabama, boycotted the segregated city bus line, winning the right to sit anywhere they chose, as well as jobs for blacks as bus drivers. Martin Luther King, Jr., a young Baptist minister in Montgomery, emerged as a leader after that boycott.

If the 1950s saw increasing opportunities for blacks, the progress that occurred during that decade went at a snail's pace compared with what happened in the 1960s. This was true in many areas of life. Musically, the 1960s were the most exciting decade of the century for blacks—in just about every area of music but jazz.

CHAPTER 8

SOUL

THE 1960s

Wilson Pickett, a major star of the 1960s, whose most famous song was probably "In the Midnight Hour," told author Gerri Hirshey about the time a young native of Liverpool, England, named Ringo Starr paid him a visit: "He said, 'Pickett?' And I didn't say nothin'. . . . So then he said, 'Wicked Pickett?' and I said, 'Yeah.' He said, 'You been singin' all around the world about a thing called soul. Can you please . . . can you pullleeeeeze tell me what it's all about?' And I said, 'Ringo. Ringo Starr,' I said; then I screamed, 'SOUUULLLLLLL!

Soul ain't nothin' but a feelin'.' He said, 'How do you know when you get it?' An' I said, 'Good God.' "

Soul came out of rhythm and blues and also out of gospel; in fact, it was closer to gospel because it was a hopeful music, a music that celebrated blackness in a way that black music had never done before. It is no accident that soul music arose in the 1960s, a period of unprecedented gains for black people and of a great surge in black pride. Beginning with the boycott of segregated buses in the late 1950s, and continuing with sit-ins at segregated lunch counters by black students in Nashville, Tennessee, and Greenville, North Carolina, in 1960, the civil rights movement spread like wildfire across the South and led to the passage of a series of federal civil rights laws that struck down at least the legal underpinnings of discrimination and segregation in America. The blacks who marched and sat in and boycotted in order to win equal rights followed the principles of nonviolence. Their leaders were predominantly ministers, such as the Reverend Martin Luther King, Jr. They were proud to have won their legal victories by moral means. The music that came to be called soul also preached a message of love.

The word *soul* was first used to describe the music of Ray Charles, the blind piano player and singer whose 1959 song "What'd I Say" was full of gospel devices, including the call-and-response pattern and even an electric piano that sounded a lot like a church organ. Jackie Wilson was another early soul artist; his songs "To Be Loved" and "Lonely Teardrops" were huge hits. But the most famous soul artist, from the early 1960s on, was James Brown—Soul Brother Number One.

James Brown

James Brown was born in a tiny shack near Barnwell, South Carolina, in 1934. His parents' marriage ended when he was four, and with his father he moved to Georgia, where Joe Brown found work in the turpentine camps that dotted the huge pine forests. James lived with his aunt in Augusta until his father found a job at a local furniture store and was able to rejoin his son. When he recognized James's musical talent, his father determined to encourage it. He managed to buy a three-legged pump organ from the store because nobody else wanted it, and he brought it home at lunchtime. By the time he returned from work that evening, a crowd had gathered around the porch to hear little James, who had never touched a keyboard before that day, play the organ.

As a teenager, Brown earned pennies dancing on street corners, shined shoes, racked pool balls, delivered groceries, and worked at anything else that could make him money. He also shoplifted, though usually for other kids. His seventh-grade teacher called him a Robin Hood who would overhear a friend complain about not having a jacket and then go out and steal one. When Brown and a group of other boys were caught breaking into cars one night, however, the Augusta police were not so charitable. Brown was neither represented by counsel nor granted bail; in 1949, when he was fifteen years old, he was sentenced to eight to sixteen years in prison.

While in prison, James Brown took stock of himself and decided that he did not want to spend the rest of his life going in and out of prison; he could make money doing what he enjoyed—performing. With a small group of fellow inmates, he formed a musical combo, using pocket combs for harmonicas and a washtub for a bass. They sang gospel music and soon were so popular that they traveled to other prisons to perform. Once, prison officials got mixed up and left the group unsupervised. Brown and the others could have escaped, but did not. When Brown applied for parole after three years, the fact that he had not tried to escape, in addition to his popularity as a prison singer, helped secure that parole for him.

Once free, Brown formed another small combo and played local clubs and dance halls, feeling lucky if he earned twenty dollars a night. Outside the prison walls, and in the places where he could get gigs, his music was primarily rhythm and blues of the raw country variety, but it had that unmistakable gospel shout. Soon, James Brown's group was opening for such artists as Little Willie John, Etta James, and Hank Ballard. But Brown wanted to be a star attraction, and that meant having a hit record. He made demonstration records, but couldn't get any record companies interested in them until finally, in 1956, King Records in Cincinnati agreed to issue his recording of "Please, Please, Please." By this time, rhythm and blues had begun to catch on with young white audiences, and "Please, Please, Please" became a huge hit, not only among blacks but also among whites. The song was two minutes and forty-two seconds of just one word—*please*—howled and shouted and panted and squealed, and it was one of the most exciting records a lot of people had ever heard.

Even more exciting was watching Brown perform live. Nobody had as much energy. He would scream into the mike, prance all over the stage, fall to his knees, then jump up and

Long before he became famous as Soul Brother Number One, with his blow-dried pompadour and self-designed costumes, James Brown made a living as best he could with small combos like this one, playing nightclubs and dance halls.

(FRANK DRIGGS COLLECTION)

spin around, and finally crash to the floor in a split. His onstage gyrations drove audiences wild, and still he kept adding more outrageous moves. The high point of Brown's show came when he would appear to collapse onstage and one of his group would come out and drape a velvet cape over his shoulders and gently lead him away. Then, just before disappearing into the wings, Brown would throw off the cape and, with an "Aahoo!" into the mike, launch into an energetic encore.

With his sprayed and blow-dried pompadour and the outfits he designed himself, James Brown was a bit much for the more genteel elements of society to take. He knew that, knew he would never be a "class act," and directed his shows and his music to "down-home" people, who of course could be found in the cities of the North as well as in the South. Songs like "I Got You (I Feel Good)," "It's a Man's, Man's, Man's World," and "Black Is Beautiful, Say It Loud: I'm Black and I'm Proud" gave voice to thoughts hidden in the hearts of many blacks, who delighted in his open, swaggering pride. In fact, by the 1960s, annoyed that black music was being overcommercialized and losing its blackness, Brown formed his own forty-member troupe, *The James Brown Show*, and played on the road for three hundred forty days in 1965.

What he lacked in education and sophistication, James Brown more than made up for in "street smarts." He was one of the first black performers to gain complete control of his own career, forming his own production company and demanding and receiving a percentage of the profits from all his performances. In 1962, he had the idea of making a live recording of his upcoming October performance at the Apollo Theater, and when King Records refused to finance the project, he financed it himself. *Live at the Apollo*, Vol. I, released in 1963, was a smash hit and stayed on the *Billboard* charts for an unprecedented sixty-six weeks.

James Brown made millions. He bought mansions, cars, clothes, and five radio stations. He also gave to and helped to raise millions for charity, which may be one reason he also acquired the nickname "the Godfather of Soul." Unfortunately, he did not give enough to the government, or so the Internal Revenue Service claimed. In the early 1970s, he was presented with a bill for four and a half million dollars in unpaid taxes for 1969 and 1970. Meanwhile, three of his radio stations failed.

It was a bad time all around. By the early 1970s, black militancy had put off many whites, and some were afraid to come to Brown's shows. Many blacks favored more commercial music. Brown's oldest son was killed in a car crash, and his second wife took their two daughters and left him. Several important members of his band left, claiming that they were overworked, underpaid, and not given enough credit. James Brown stopped touring and essentially dropped out for about eight years. By the late 1970s, there were a lot of young people in America who had never even heard of James Brown, though he was still enormously popular in Europe.

It was English groups like The Clash and the Rolling Stones who helped revive interest in James Brown by mentioning him as an influence on them. James Brown, after seeming to turn his back on the outside world and admit to defeat, found the energy to make his own comeback. He has produced albums on his own record label and has taken advantage of the revival of interest in the music of the 1960s by again forming a touring show. In 1980, he appeared in the movie *The Blues Brothers*, starring Dan Aykroyd and John Belushi. He is credited with influencing many younger performers: When Michael Jackson was very young, his onstage performance was a carbon copy of James Brown's. Brown cut the first rap record, "America Is My Home," long before Grandmaster Flash and the Furious Five ever thought about rap recordings. By the mid-1980s, he was fifty and feeling it, so he had no plans to try to re-create his electrifying stage performances of the 1960s, but the passing years had done nothing to diminish his pride. He knew he was a pioneer.

While James Brown had diehard fans among whites, neither he nor any other down-home soul singer captured a major share of the white market in the 1960s. But a greater number of black singers did manage the crossover during that decade; in fact, at times they practically eclipsed white singers on the pop record charts. As Ted Fox, author of *Showtime at the Apollo*, puts it, "America had become sweet on black music. At the beginning of the rhythm-and-blues era, there were almost no black-oriented radio stations. By 1967 there were a hundred stations primarily playing black music—even though only five of the stations were owned by blacks. Hundreds of other pop-oriented stations also included many black records on their playlists. As the restrictions of segregation began to crumble thanks to the civil-rights movement, black music recorded by black artists became big business."

The word *sweet* is important in Fox's statement, for in nearly all cases the popular records were a very commercialized and sweetened version of rhythm and blues, and especially at the beginning of the 1960s, the most popular black artists were girl groups—the Chantels, the Angels, Rosie and the Originals, the Crystals, the Shirelles. Also, while the artists were black, their producers and managers were white. But when the decade was still young, an enterprising black man in Detroit named Berry Gordy, Jr., showed that with the right formula and plenty of eager young talent, a black company could dominate the pop charts in America. So many of the acts that he produced became famous that it is impossible to select just one, and since they were all part of the same record company "family," the star was the company itself—Motown.

Motown

Berry Gordy began his adult life as an assembly-line worker for the Ford Motor Company, but his real love was music, especially jazz. In 1955, he opened his own jazz record store, but he had misjudged the record market. Rock 'n' roll was the kind of music people were buying, and the store went broke within a year. Gordy then began to write rock 'n' roll songs. He wrote "Lonely Teardrops," which was released in 1958 and was one of the hits that made Jackie Wilson famous. But in merely writing songs, Gordy was still working for other people, and he wanted to be his own boss. He became an independent producer, signing up his own talent, making demonstration records, and then leasing those records to music companies. He found his talent right in Detroit, and was extremely fortunate to meet up with a young singer and song-writer named William "Smokey" Robinson, whose group, the

Miracles, was the first that Gordy recorded. He leased that record to Chess, a black company in Chicago. He also signed up a young singer named Marvin Gaye and leased his record to United Artists.

The next step was to form his own record company, which he did in 1959 with a loan of eight hundred dollars and a lot of nerve. (The history of small, independent black record companies is not notable for its successes, and there were no other record companies at all in Detroit, which was best known for making cars, not music.) Gordy called his company Hitsville, USA. Within a few months, he had signed up such groups as the Marvelettes, the Contours, and the Primes, whose name was changed to the Temptations, and such individuals as Mary Wells and a nine-year-old blind boy named Stevie Morris, who later became known as Little Stevie Wonder. For every group or individual Gordy signed, he turned dozens of others away. Detroit's black neighborhoods were bursting with talent, but Hitsville was a small company, and Gordy decided that he had better concentrate on just a few acts. One group that he turned away were the Primettes, the sister group of the Primes, because the girls were still in high school and unable to devote the necessary time to singing careers. He did sign them after graduation and changed their name to the Supremes.

Berry Gordy realized that talent alone was not enough. His groups had to have a marketable sound, and in the early 1960s that meant music that had a steady, driving, very danceable beat and catchy, youthful lyrics about love. Smokey Robinson seemed to know exactly how to achieve that sound, and he wrote many of the company's early songs. Berry Gordy also realized that the presentation of those songs was important to their popularity, and he spent as much time grooming his young acts for the stage as he did developing material for them. In fact, signing a contract with Hitsville, USA was tantamount to signing one's life away. Each act was carefully costumed and choreographed and taught that a solid dose of showmanship was essential to success. In the early days, Hitsville, USA acts played only small local theaters, but the performers dressed and went through their intricately choreographed movements as if they were entertaining the president. Gordy's attention to detail and his emphasis on professionalism soon paid off—in 1962, Hitsville had no less than five hit records: "Do You Love Me?" by the Contours, "Beechwood 4–5789" and "Please, Mr. Postman" by the Marvelettes, and "The One Who Really Loves You" and "You Beat Me to the Punch" by Mary Wells. That same year, Gordy changed the name of his company to Motown, a contraction of Motor Town, Detroit's nickname because of its importance in the automobile industry. By the following year, the name Motown was on the lips of everyone in the music industry and the Motown sound was the one to copy.

In 1963, Martha and the Vandellas had two big hits ("Heat Wave" and "Come and Get These Memories"), the Miracles had one with "You've Really Got a Hold on Me," and Little Stevie Wonder played his harmonica and sang his way to number one on the charts with "Fingertips."

In 1962, Gordy had finally signed the Primettes (after they had graduated from high school), changed their name to the Supremes, and seen to it that they had lessons in etiquette and elegant gowns and wigs while he worked to find just the right songs for them. He also experimented with different lead singers in the group and decided that although Mary Wilson had been the lead singer, Diana Ross had a voice that was more "commercial." With Ross singing lead, the Supremes hit the top of the charts in 1964 with "Where Did Our Love Go?" In the next five years, they had eleven more number-one pop hits and became Motown's greatest commercial success. Not only did they successfully make the crossover to the white juvenile audience, they also appealed to white adults, for they were smooth and polished and there was never a hint of raunchiness in their songs. In 1966, they were the first Motown group to play the Copacabana, one of New York City's most sophisticated nightclubs.

Berry Gordy often referred to his company as the Motown "family," and indeed it was a very closely knit group. Many of the acts were brought to the company by other acts: Ronnie White of the Miracles brought Little Stevie Wonder to Berry Gordy's attention. The Supremes gained entree because they had been the sister group to the Temptations. Both Diana Ross and Gladys Knight (of Gladys Knights and the Pips) claim to have discovered the Jackson Five. Marvin Gaye married Berry Gordy's sister Anna. Jermaine Jackson married Berry Gordy's daughter Hazel.

The Jackson Five were the last highly successful group in the long string of Motown successes that began in 1962. Their first single for Motown, "I Want You Back," featuring eleven-year-old Michael Jackson singing a love song to a girl, was released in 1969 and reached the top of the charts. It was followed by "ABC," which won the group their first Grammy Award in 1970.

Berry Gordy was once asked to define the Detroit, or Motown, sound, and so he and Smokey Robinson and others sat around and tried to come up with an answer. "We thought of the neighborhoods we were raised in," he later explained, "and came up with a six-word definition: 'Rats, roaches, struggle, talent, guts, love.' " There were elements of gospel, rhythm and blues, and soul in the Motown songs—more in the beat and the manner of singing than in the lyrics. There were some highly talented songwriters at the company, including Nick Ashford and Valerie Simpson and the trio who wrote most of the songs for the Supremes—Brian and Eddie Holland and Lamont Dozier. And, of course, there were all those talented and energetic young performers.

But the key to the success of the Motown sound probably lies partly in the fact that, though it was black, it was not too black. At a time when many whites, especially young whites, wanted to appreciate black people and their music, a sound that was not too far away from their own experience was the most acceptable. Neither Motown's music nor its image was ever in the least bit threatening to whites. Berry Gordy stayed out of politics and made sure that his performers did, too. The only reason the Supremes took to wearing Afro wigs, for example, was because the style was "in" from the middle 1960s on—in no way were they making any sort of "black is beautiful" statement. In the summer of 1967, blacks rioted in Detroit's ghetto neighborhoods. A Motown revue happened to be performing in the city at the time and it fled immediately. Motown was not going to be associated with black riots. In early 1972, a reporter asked the Jackson Five if they had done anything for the movement to win civil rights for black people.

The Motown publicist who was with the boys—there was always a Motown publicist at hand when a Motown performer was interviewed—interrupted to assure the reporter that they were not active in any movements.

Some people have suggested that one reason Motown's influence had waned by the early 1970s is that it lacked relevance to what was going on in the country. But that is probably an unfair charge. Just because a black company is successful does not mean that it has a duty to crusade for black rights. Many other black performers were active in the civil rights movement, but they were much more aware of what was going on outside the world of music than the Motown performers were. Diana Ross remembers being so wrapped up in recording and touring that she didn't have time to read the newspapers, even if she had wanted to.

Indeed, there was something cocoonlike about the Motown family, and eventually that worked against the company. Berry Gordy insisted on such tight control that many of his long-standing acts began to chafe under it: By the late 1960s to early 1970s, many left the company, including Gladys Knight and the Pips, the Temptations, the Jackson Five, and eventually even Diana Ross.

At the same time, Berry Gordy had become interested in the movie business—he moved to Los Angeles in 1969—and in the course of devoting himself to that seems to have lost his usually keen sense of changing trends in the record business: By the end of the 1960s, albums had replaced singles in popularity, and people who bought albums wanted lots of original songs on them. Motown was still concentrating on singles, and its albums still included a lot of "covers," or renditions of songs that had already been recorded by other artists. The Motown songwriting team of Holland-Dozier-Holland had broken up, and that was difficult for the company. Also, a more hard-edged and sophisticated "Philadelphia sound," exemplified by Sly and the Family Stone, was now challenging the traditional Motown formula. By the early 1970s, the Motown domination of the pop charts had ended, but the company hardly disappeared into the mist. Stevie Wonder and Smokey Robinson stayed, and in the 1970s and 1980s the Commodores, Lionel Richie, and Stephanie Mills have had big hits. The company has also branched out and signed white performers. Motown, and Berry Gordy, remain a power in the music industry.

Aretha!

No chapter on black music—or music, period—in the 1960s would be complete without mentioning Aretha Franklin. Her hit song "Respect," released in the late 1960s, became a kind of rallying cry for many sixties activists—not just blacks, but also the women of the fledgling women's liberation movement. Her records also sparked a revival of gospel music, for Franklin's brand of soul was straight out of the church. Coincidentally, she grew up in Detroit, but her sound was far away from that of Motown.

Aretha Franklin was born March 25, 1942, the second of six children of the Reverend C. L. Franklin. Her mother left the family when Aretha was six and died four years later. None other than the great gospel singer Mahalia Jackson became a kind of substitute mother to the children, and when Franklin showed singing talent at a young age, her first forum was naturally the church. She sang her first solo in her father's Detroit church when she was ten and by age fourteen was a full-fledged evangelistic singer, traveling around the Midwest singing in various churches. Her voice enthralled her audiences, and perhaps the adults around her decided that if she could sing so convincingly about God, she didn't need a human chaperone. She was left essentially on her own, and it wasn't long before she got into trouble. By age seventeen, she'd had two children out of wedlock, and by age eighteen, she has said, she had lived "more than most people do in a lifetime."

When Franklin was eighteen, she went against the wishes of Mahalia Jackson and joined the blues circuit populated by Lou Rawls, Mavis Staples, Sam Cooke, and the Soul Circuit, all of whom sang a sort of commercialized, wordly gospel. Her father approved the change and took her to New York to be closer to the major record companies; he then went back to Detroit, leaving her to her own devices. A musician and would-be manager named Jo King took Franklin under her wing and secured a contract for her with Columbia Records. She had a minor hit for the company with "You Made Me Love You," but she resented the company's insistence that she sing pop music when she wanted to sing blues and her own gospel compositions. Still, she stayed with Columbia, though she soon left King's management for that of Ted White, whom she married in 1962 when she was twenty.

In 1966, after six years, ten albums, and many singles for Columbia, Franklin had only a couple of minor hits, and she still wasn't singing the material with which she felt most comfortable. Her husband helped her to get a contract with Atlantic Records, and a producer there, Jerry Wexler, recognized her special gifts and promised to let her show them.

Wexler took Franklin to Muscle Shoals, Alabama, to the Fame recording studios, where he had assembled a group of musicians who specialized in down-home rhythm and blues. Half of them were white—and for that matter so was Wexler—but Franklin lost her suspicions about what she was getting into when she was invited to sit down at the piano and tool around with the musicians. After she felt comfortable, they started working on a new song by Ronny Shannon called "I Never Loved a Man (the Way I Love You)." Aretha liked the bluesy lyrics (the man in question is a mean heartbreaker, a liar, and a thief), but she especially liked the fact that she was allowed to sing them the way she wanted to—and that was with all the gospel gusto that she could muster. The record was released by Atlantic in February 1967, and sold a quarter of a million copies in the first two weeks. Soon, it had sold a million copies and was judged "gold."

Four days after the release of the single, Franklin was at work on her first album for Atlantic—in a New York recording studio this time, but with basically the same crew that had been with her in Muscle Shoals. Also titled *I Never Loved a Man*, it contained a song that had been written and first sung by a young soul singer named Otis Redding, called "Respect." The song had a very simple lyric—basically, the word sung over and over, and even spelled out. Its impact depended a lot on its presentation, and what a presentation Aretha Franklin gave it! No doubt she was reminded of her own personal problems (which she still had, since she and her husband Ted

White were not getting along and would be divorced the following year), and perhaps she was also thinking of how hard it was to be black, and a woman, when she sang the song. Whatever she was thinking, she sang that song like it was the soul declaration of independence.

"Respect" blew the top off the charts. It was number one in black urban neighborhoods, which also happened to be the scenes of riots that summer—in fact, in some black neighborhoods the summer of 1967 was known as the summer of " 'Retha, rap, and revolt." It also made the all-important cross-over to the white audience and soon became the unofficial anthem of the women's liberation movement. In colleges across the country, white coeds talked about Aretha as if they were good friends, and in fact from then on Aretha Franklin didn't need to be identified by any last name—there was only one Aretha.

Many of Franklin's next hits had very simple lyrics that diverse groups of people could identify with. "Think" consisted primarily of Franklin screaming the word *freedom* while a background girl chorus alternated with the admonition "Think about it." "Chain of Fools" was not about the war in Vietnam, but it caught on with the troops over there. There may have been a method behind the choice of songs, and Jerry Wexler, who became something of a music world celebrity in his own right because of his "discovery" of Franklin, may have had something to do with it. Whatever, it worked.

Wexler and Atlantic Records remained true to their promise to allow Franklin to record what she wanted, and in 1972 she recorded a double gospel album at New Temple Missionary Baptist Church in Los Angeles. One of the cuts, the traditional

157

A young Aretha Franklin, recently arrived in New York, takes lessons from choreographer Cholly Atkins in performing the songs she's recording for Columbia Records. (FRANK DRIGGS COLLECTION)

gospel hymn "Amazing Grace," went gold, possibly the first—
and the last to date—gospel song to do so.

By the early 1970s, musical tastes had changed again. Now
the big sounds were disco and hard rock. Franklin tried, but
could not find, a place for herself, though she experimented
with many different sounds. Eventually, she left Atlantic Records. She also moved to Los Angeles and decided to study
acting. There she met the actor Glynn Turman, whom she
married in 1979. There she also got a part in the film *The
Blues Brothers*, starring Dan Aykroyd and John Belushi. The
same year as the film was released, Franklin signed a contract
with Arista Records, and in 1983, with her third album for
that company, *Jump to It*, she made it back to the charts and
started excited talk among Franklin fans of an Aretha comeback. The possible comeback became a reality with her next
album, *Who's Zoomin' Who*, containing the hit singles of the
title song and "Freeway of Love." In her forties by that time,
the woman who as an eighteen-year-old had already lived
more than most people do in a lifetime felt as if she had been
musically born again.

The 1960s were a time of great turmoil in the United States.
They were a time of movements—they began with the civil
rights movement, continued with the antiwar movement, and
ended with the women's liberation movement. They were a
time of great activity in the music world as well. Two distinct
areas of the music world benefited most. One was white folk
music—the lyrics of Bob Dylan and Joan Baez, for example,
became rallying cries for the antiwar crusaders. But there was
not, and never has been, a lot of emotion in the *sound* of folk
music. That was supplied by the music of black people—soul.

CHAPTER 9

NEW DIRECTIONS

THE 1970s AND TODAY

Many people do not consider the mid-1970s to the mid-1980s
a very important era in the history of black music. Since we
are dealing with recent history, and since it is hard to judge
recent history with the same objectivity as past history, these
people may prove to be wrong. We may look back one day
and decide that the mid-1970s to the mid-1980s were in fact
an important time in black music history. But at least right
now, these years are regarded as a time when many black
music makers found that for one reason or another they were
out of style, and so stepped back and worked quietly on their

music and privately began to develop the sounds that became so exciting in the mid-1980s.

Starting in the mid-1970s, the public turned away from soul and toward hard rock, whose chief practitioners were white and male. Album-oriented rock (AOR) became popular, and many music radio stations started playing AOR and no black music at all. The Top 30 and Top 40 lists were no longer as integrated. From 1960 to 1964, the *Billboard* Top 30 list included twenty-seven records by black artists; from 1970 to 1974, the number was thirty-five; from 1980 to 1984, it was only fifteen. Videos, the musical phenomenon of the 1980s, were from the beginning primarily white and hard rock; MTV's 1984 video awards ballot contained fewer than forty black entries out of 677.

All this is not to say that black music and black musicians and singers fell by the wayside altogether. But black music lost the mass appeal that it had enjoyed. Says rock critic and author Dave Marsh, "In the '60s, we had the doors [to integrated music] wide open. Our mistake was being so naive we didn't think to take them off the hinges." Part of the reason for this loss of mass appeal may have been "backlash"—whites feeling that blacks had cornered the music market long enough. Part of it was the natural change in public taste—no musical style lasts forever.

A major reason, however, was changes in the record business itself. Once albums became more popular than singles, production costs soared, and small, independent labels like the kind Motown had once been could not compete with the major labels. One week in the summer of 1984, ninety-nine of the records on the *Billboard* Hot 100 were recorded on major labels. Since many blacks record on independent labels, this trend was bound to affect them. Even blacks who did record for major labels found that they did not get as much promotion as white stars who recorded for the same labels. And promotion was everything. Major record companies had huge promotion networks, but they were aimed primarily at the white market—white radio stations, white TV talk shows and variety shows, and concerts (which are also regarded as "white" because black fans are not as concert-oriented as white fans, probably because they do not have as much money to spend on tickets). Any black entertainer who was successful managed to make the crossover to the white market. There were plenty who did.

One was Donna Summer, who reigned for a time as "the Queen of Disco." Disco arose from Latin music roots, but quickly came to be associated with black music. In fact, the term came to be used as an all-purpose name for black music in the 1970s, just as rhythm and blues and soul have been used. Summer, a young, black American singer who had been living and performing in Europe since 1968, returned to her native country in 1976 with the smash disco hit "Love to Love You, Baby." Two years later, she appeared in a Motown-produced movie called *Thank God It's Friday* in which she sang the song "Last Dance." The song won not only the 1979 Academy Award for best song in a motion picture, but the award for favorite disco single at the American Music Awards; and Donna herself won a Grammy Award for best female vocal for her performance of the song.

In 1979, Donna Summer went through a religious conversion and became a born-again Christian. She stopped singing disco songs and turned to music that was less sexy and suggestive; by doing so, she discovered her own "soul" and had a major hit in the early 1980s in "She Works Hard for the Money," a hard-driving rhythm and blues song. Also during the 1980s, Donna Summer recorded an album of country music, which was a breakthrough of sorts, for except for Charley Pride, almost everyone who sang or played country music was white (which still is so as of this writing).

It is interesting to note that the majority of black stars in the 1970s and 1980s have been veteran performers who had their first big successes in the golden days of the 1960s and early 1970s and later managed to survive the backlash and changes in musical taste by maturing and changing with the times. Diana Ross went through a lot of changes in the 1970s; first she left the Supremes and began a career as a single, and later she left Motown. Lionel Richie, who had spent ten years as a member of the Commodores, also took the big step of going out on his own; as a single, he moved from being a "black artist" and made the crossover to enormous success in the pop (white) market.

Stevie Wonder grew up during the 1970s, maturing from a cute and talented blind kid into a creative and talented musician-singer-songwriter. While he remained with Motown, he asked for and received an unprecedented amount of creative control—he could write and produce his own material. The albums Wonder began to produce in the early 1970s showed that he could handle all the control he was given. In 1974, he made music history by being nominated for six Grammy awards (more than anyone else before) and then being awarded five of the six Grammys for which he had been nominated: album of the year (*Innervisions*), best-engineered recording ("Superstition"), best pop vocal performance ("Superstition"), best rhythm and blues single ("Superstition"), and best pop vocal performance by a male singer ("You Are the Sunshine of My Life").

Evident on these records was Wonder's creative use of the comparatively new music synthesizers, which were beginning to make big changes in the music world. Using a synthesizer, one can re-create the sound of just about any instrument and record many, many tracks for a song. Stevie Wonder is ingenious in his use of the new musical technologies, and has used them to their best advantage in all his albums since the 1970s. He has also done a great deal of work in other areas of new technology—especially computers. He has worked closely with companies that are developing voice recorders and braille music readers. And he has used his talent and fame in many areas outside music. He wrote a song to commemorate the birthday of Martin Luther King, Jr., and worked very hard in the successful campaign to get King's birthday declared a national holiday. He has spoken out on international causes; in 1985, he performed at the United Nations. Many of the songs he has written have been recorded by major orchestras such as the New York Philharmonic. Once billed as a twelve-year-old genius, he is now regarded as a musical genius by most people who really know about music.

Tina Turner found herself and her own special sound in the early 1980s. Twenty years earlier, she and her husband, Ike Turner, had been major stars, but by the mid-1970s, they and their sound were out of fashion and they were reduced to playing a lot of one-night stands in small towns. That had not helped their relationship, which had always been rocky, despite the fact that they had been together for twenty years. There had been violence and extramarital affairs on Ike's part, and finally in the middle of a tour in Texas in 1976, Tina walked out with nothing but thirty-six cents and a Mobil credit card. Later, Ike sent Tina her clothes, which was all she wanted, although she had every right to half of the wealth they had accumulated together. She lived on food stamps and played small black clubs for three years until she got a manager who decided that she had an audience in young white rock fans. He started booking Turner into rock clubs. Her big break came in 1981 when the Rolling Stones asked her to tour with them. Then Rod Stewart asked her to appear on his TV special.

Still, Turner could not get a record contract in the United States. Aware that British performers appreciated her most, Turner's manager decided that she would find a more welcoming audience abroad, and in the early 1980s she performed mostly in Poland, Hungary, and Yugoslavia, as well as in Teheran, Iran. Then, in 1982, an English band called Heaven 17 asked Turner to record an old Temptations song for an album and a video they were doing, and she became the first black female to appear on MTV.

Finally, in 1982, she got a contract with Capitol Records, and in 1984 she recorded her first album in ten years, *Private Dancer*. Not only the album but also the single "What's Love Got to Do With It" was a smash hit. Turner won a Grammy for the single and three Grammys for the album: *The New York Times* called *Private Dancer* a landmark in the evolution of pop-soul music. At the age of forty-six or so (Tina Turner does not like to tell her age), she was a major star in her own right. She had managed the all-important crossover, and it was not just because of her music. The fact that at her age she could make such an astonishing comeback, and still look so good and perform with such sensuality, appealed to a lot of people, young and old, black and white. Turner was the hottest female singer in the country.

Michael Jackson

The greatest 1960s-to-1980s success story is that of Michael Jackson, born in 1958 and a star when he was only eleven years old. During the 1970s, he became a teenager and his voice changed. Suddenly, he could not depend on it hitting the notes he wanted it to reach. Since he had been the lead singer on most of the Jackson Five's big hits, this was a serious situation. At the same time, Motown was changing—artists were leaving, the successful songwriting team of Holland-Dozier-Holland broke up, and Berry Gordy was paying more attention to his film company than to his music company. The Jackson brothers were writing songs and wanted to record them; they also wanted to help produce their albums. Motown did not want them to have that kind of creative control.

In 1976, the Jackson Five left Motown and signed with Epic Records; but Motown retained the right to their name. The group became The Jacksons, and with the move from Motown they lost Jermaine, who married Berry Gordy's daughter and decided to remain with his father-in-law's company. With Epic, the brothers enjoyed more creative control, and their first Epic album, *Enjoy Yourself*, released in 1976, went gold, as did the single of the same name. Three years later, they had another gold album, *Destiny*, and another gold single, "Shake Your Body (Down to the Ground)." By the time *Destiny* was released, however, Michael had turned twenty and was eager to go out on his own. While he continued to record with his brothers, he wanted to make his own albums.

Actually, Michael Jackson had recorded albums of his own since the Motown days. But now he wanted to write and produce his own material. Aware that he did not have either the experience or the expertise to do it all himself, he asked producer-performer-songwriter Quincy Jones to produce his first solo album for CBS. The result was *Off the Wall*. Released in 1979, it went gold. By early 1980, it had made music history, for it was the first solo record album ever to produce four Top 10 hits: "Don't Stop 'Til You Get Enough," "Rock With You," "She's Out of My Life," and "Off the Wall." But that was nothing compared with what happened with his next solo album, *Thriller*.

Once again, Jackson and Quincy Jones worked together to select the songs, plan the instrumentation, and lay down the tracks for each cut. This time, Jackson, who is very much against racial segregation in music or in any other area, wanted to put some integration into the album. He had recorded a song with Paul McCartney called "The Girl Is Mine," and they both included it on their new albums. Jackson also asked hard-rock guitarist Eddie Van Halen to play on the cut "Beat It." The rock group Toto played backup on several other cuts. The album was released in late 1982 and almost immediately started to make music history. By early March 1983, it was number one, and it was still in the Top 10 in June 1984. When it reached sales of twenty-five million copies worldwide, it went into the *Guinness Book of World Records* as the all-time best-selling solo record album. Meanwhile, various cuts from the album had been released as singles. All together, six cuts were smash hits (there were only nine songs on the album), and that was also a record number. At the Grammy Awards presentation in 1984, Jackson won an unprecedented eight awards; people called that Grammy Awards ceremony "the Michael Jackson Show."

Jackson filmed videos of several of the album cuts. His "Billie Jean" video, which was first aired on MTV in March 1983, was the first video by a black artist to be played as often as videos by white artists. His "Thriller" video was the first video ever actually purchased by MTV (all earlier videos had been given to MTV free of charge as promotions to sell records, just as records are given to radio stations). At the first MTV Video Music Awards in September 1984, Jackson won three awards, more than anyone else and, obviously, more than any other black entertainer.

Michael Jackson blazed trails for black entertainers. After his videos were so successful on MTV, MTV started showing videos by Prince, Sylvester, Bob Marley, and other blacks. Jackson also did more for the record industry in general than any other performer, black or white, had in a long time. Record sales had not been very good in the early 1980s. The disco craze had died down, and nothing had come along to take its place. When *Thriller* was released, people who wanted to buy it had to go into record stores. While there, they looked around and often bought other records, too. The whole record industry was indebted to Michael Jackson.

After *Thriller*, Jackson paid what he considered an outstanding debt to his family by recording an album with his brothers called *Victory* and accompanying them on a nationwide performing tour. Once that was over, he turned once again to his own career. He was involved in many different projects. One was a short film for Walt Disney Productions. He was also writing songs and preparing a new album. He took time out to write, with Lionel Richie, the song "We Are the World," which was recorded by a large cast of singers, black and white, to benefit USA for Africa, an organization formed to help the starving people in Ethiopia. Only in his twenties, Michael Jackson still had his life ahead of him, and there was no telling what he would create in the coming years, or what his final place in the history of American music would be.

Quincy Jones

One man whose place in American and black music history is assured is Quincy Jones, who produced both of Michael Jackson's smash-hit solo albums. Long a behind-the-scenes artist—a producer, mixer, writer, arranger, and conductor— Jones has become a star in his own right and can pick and choose the projects on which he works. He belongs in the tradition of William Grant Still, and no overview of black music in the second half of the twentieth century would be complete without a section on him.

He was born Quincy Delightt Jones in 1933 on the South Side of Chicago, which at the time was full of jazz musicians. But when he was ten, his father and stepmother moved their family of nine children to a suburb of Seattle, Washington, and oddly enough it was there that Quincy experienced his first strong musical influences. He met Joseph Pole, who had a band that played exciting arrangements. "I used to baby-sit for Joe Pole so I could look over his orchestration books," recalls Jones. "I was really hung up on horns. . . . I started to play trumpet and I wanted to write music from the very first day." He also met Ray Charles, the blind pianist-singer who was just three years older than he. They jammed together and eventually formed a combo that played at local dances and in small clubs.

When Jones was fifteen, he heard that Lionel Hampton was going to be appearing in Seattle with his orchestra; he approached Hampton and showed him a suite he had written called *The Four Winds*. Not only did Hampton play the piece, but he invited the youngster to join the band. Jones accepted immediately, but Hampton's wife and manager, Gladys, wouldn't hear of taking a kid out of school. She insisted that Jones graduate from high school first.

By the time he graduated from high school, Jones had decided to get as much formal training as he could. He attended the Berklee College of Music in Boston on scholarship, playing trumpet nights and weekends at local strip joints. From there, he went to New York and at last joined Lionel Hampton's band. With Hampton he went on an international tour in 1957 and remained in Europe when the band went home. He studied musical composition in Paris and served as musical director at a Paris music studio. He then went to Stockholm, Sweden, where he became musical director of *Free and Easy*, an opera written by the American composer Harold Arlen, which toured Europe in 1959 and 1960.

After *Free and Easy* closed, Jones formed a big band from among its musicians and toured both Europe and the United

Around 1961 Quincy Jones went to work as music director for Mercury Records in New York. In 1964 he became a vice president, the first black ever to hold such a high office in a white-owned record company. (FRANK DRIGGS COLLECTION)

States in 1960 and 1961. The cost of supporting eighteen musicians and their families proved too high, and the band broke up. Jones went to work as music director at Mercury Records in New York and in 1964 was named a vice president, thus becoming the first black ever to hold such a high executive office in a white-owned record company. But he was not one to stay in an office, pushing papers. He produced albums, often sat in with the orchestra during recording sessions, and wrote music and arrangements for many recording artists, including Frank Sinatra, Sammy Davis, Jr., Andy Williams, Sarah Vaughan, Peggy Lee, and Aretha Franklin.

Meanwhile, also in 1964, Jones composed the music for his first Hollywood film, *The Pawnbroker*, directed by Sidney Lumet, who had invited him to write the score. Months passed before he scored his second Hollywood film, *Mirage*, for Universal, which was released in 1965; but after that he was in constant demand in Hollywood. Many of the theme songs Jones wrote for movies became hits, and two of them—"For Love of Ivy" and "The Eyes of Love"—were nominated for Academy Awards in the best song category. His score for the film *In Cold Blood* was also nominated. In 1971, he arranged and conducted the music for the Academy Awards presentation. He also wrote the theme songs for a variety of TV programs, including *Ironside, Sanford and Son*, and *The Bill Cosby Show*. In fact, Jones had so much film work that he did not have the time to be a record company executive. In 1968, he left Mercury Records.

The following year, Jones signed as a recording artist with A&M Records. His first A&M album, *Walking in Space*, won the Grammy for best jazz instrumental album. His second,

Gula Matari, won a Grammy for best instrumental composition and best instrumental arrangement the following year. The next year, 1971, his third album, *Smackwater Jack*, won the Grammy for best instrumental pop, rock, or folk performance.

Even an energetic and prodigious talent like Quincy Jones's could not keep up such a pace for long. By 1973, he was turning out nine film scores a year, in addition to his other work, and felt like "a machine." He decided to stop working in Hollywood and devote himself to performing. He formed a temporary big band to work with singer Roberta Flack at two concerts at the Felt Forum in New York. He also recorded the album *You've Got It Bad, Girl*, on which he made his debut as a singer; the single of the same title was a hit throughout the summer of 1973.

In August 1974, blood vessels leading to Jones's brain burst, a condition that usually results in death. Fortunately, surgeons were able to repair the blood vessels in two operations, and Jones was back at work in six months, though with several metal plates in his head and a scar on his forehead. He was also a different man mentally and emotionally. Having come so close to death, he had acquired a different attitude about life, and about his music. Long regarded as primarily a jazz musician, he turned more to pop in his next album, *Body Heat*, saying that it was "not a jazz album per se, it was a music album in which I tried to express the music that I feel." *Body Heat* contained a wide range of musical styles, and not only was it artistically satisfying for Jones, it was also commercially successful. It sold over a million copies and remained in the top five on the charts for over six months.

Jones was also at work on an eighty-minute composition that traced the evolution of black American music from its African origins to the present. Coincidentally, he was asked to write the score for the twelve-hour ABC-TV film *Roots*, and he drew heavily on his own composition for that work; his score for *Roots* is probably the most personal film score he has ever written.

Jones has continued to be the busiest black man in the music world. In addition to Michael Jackson's record-breaking albums, he has in recent years produced albums for Roberta Flack, Patti Austin, and Frank Sinatra. He produced the album *We Are the World*, recorded by a host of American artists to aid Ethiopian famine victims. His next major project was collaborating on the score of the film version of Alice Walker's Pulitzer Prize–winning novel, *The Color Purple*, directed by Steven Spielberg. Though in his early fifties, and having been through a life-threatening illness, Jones has no intentions of slowing down. The musical ideas keep coming, and he must follow them. In doing so, he gives America, and the world, some of the most memorable music of recent times.

If one considers when Quincy Jones was born (1933), it seems clear that only an exceptional talent could have managed to obtain the formal training and the many opportunities he has enjoyed. Black Americans were still discriminated against when Jones was growing up, and generally had few chances for formal musical training or higher education of any kind. Even the most talented musical directors had little hope of becoming record-company executives or composers of Hollywood film scores. But the 1960s were a time when opportunities for blacks opened up in many areas, and though times and attitudes have changed since then, that decade has left a legacy—life for black Americans has not gone back to the way it was before the 1960s.

Blacks who were born in the 1960s had opportunities that their parents could only have dreamed about, and many of them have thrived with those opportunities. They also have felt that it is their right to refuse to be categorized as black, especially in the fields of music and literature. Michael Jackson, for example, does not like the fact that his music is categorized as "black music." He does not understand why his 1979 album *Off the Wall* was nominated for a 1980 Grammy only in the rhythm and blues category—why not in the pop category? For that reason, he refused to sing at any future Grammy Awards presentations, including the 1984 awards night when he was nominated for so many Grammys.

Wynton Marsalis questions why jazz, as "black music," is considered less technically demanding than the European classical music of Bach and Debussy. In his opinion, jazz is far *more* technically demanding than classical music and he should know, since he was the first person—not just black person, but *person*—to win Grammy awards in both jazz and classical music on the same night.

So far, this chapter has not focused on jazz in the mid-1970s to the mid-1980s, which is not to say that nothing was happening in the jazz world. There were new developments. One of the most notable was the transition to what is called "jazz-rock," led by Miles Davis, guitarist Larry Coryell, and others, and evident in the music of the groups Chicago and Blood, Sweat & Tears. Another was the work of the Chicago-based Association for the Advancement of Creative Musicians (AACM), which was formed in the mid-1960s and was strongly influencing young jazz musicians in the 1970s. Twenty years from now, music historians may be able to put more concrete labels on these developments, and these developments may be considered extremely important in jazz, and American music history.

As of this writing, however, jazz is not a major influence in American musical trends. It is overshadowed by more popular, more commercial music because it is generally regarded as music that is hard to understand. As such, it shares much with contemporary classical music, which also does not sell a lot of records or pack people into concert halls across America the way a pop music star does. What it does not share with contemporary classical music is its racial identification. The new classical music is considered white, and may be hard for the average listener to appreciate because it seems highbrow and intellectual; whereas jazz is considered black, and may be hard for the general listener to appreciate because it grew out of ghettos and red-light districts, which places it at a distance from the experience of the average middle-class citizen.

Until the 1980s, there was no one musician, white or black, who was capable of challenging that racial division in technically difficult music. That is why the young Wynton Marsalis is so famous now, and why he may prove to be very important in the history of black music in America.

Wynton Marsalis

Wynton Marsalis was born in 1961 in New Orleans, the cradle of jazz, and also into a highly musical family. His father, Ellis Marsalis, was a jazz musician and teacher. His mother, Dolores, had sung for a time with jazz groups. Their first son, Branford, showed talent on the clarinet and piano by the time he was in second grade, and that led Ellis Marsalis to believe that Wynton, the second of his six sons, might also be musically talented. At the time, Ellis Marsalis was playing with the band of Al Hirt, the celebrated white New Orleans trumpet player. He asked Hirt for an advance on his salary in order to buy six-year-old Wynton a trumpet. Hirt did not give him the money; instead, he gave Wynton one of his own trumpets. Wynton appreciated the gift and took courses in trumpet at the Xavier Junior School of Music, but he was more interested in baseball and Boy Scouts than in trumpet playing.

When he was twelve, however, Marsalis heard a recording by the great jazz trumpet player Clifford Brown. He was so enthralled by the idea of making those kinds of sounds on the trumpet that he started really practicing. Under John Longo, a trumpet player who knew both jazz and classical styles, he grew equally interested in the classical possibilities of the trumpet, especially in the work of Maurice André, a French classical trumpeter.

Young Wynton determined to be the best trumpet player he could be, and he used every spare minute he had to practice. In addition to studying with Longo, he took courses in theory and harmony at the New Orleans Center for the Creative Arts. At the age of fourteen, he won a statewide classical competition and as a result was invited to be a featured soloist with the New Orleans Philharmonic Orchestra. During his high school years, he played with the New Orleans Civic Orchestra, the New Orleans Brass Quintet, and the Creators, a teenage funk rock group in which his older brother, Branford, played saxophone.

By the time Marsalis was seventeen, his talent was so apparent that the Berkshire Music Center at Tanglewood, in Massachusetts, waived its normal age requirement (eighteen) so he could attend its summer session. He won its Harvey Shapiro Award as the outstanding brass player. His instructors were amazed by his versatility. They had never met a seventeen-year-old who could play both classical and jazz music so well, and who could move so effortlessly from a demanding classical piece to a demanding jazz piece.

On graduating from high school, Marsalis, who had maintained a 3.98 (out of a possible 4.0) grade-point average and was a National Merit Scholarship finalist, had scholarship offers from Yale University and other Ivy League schools as well as from the Juilliard School of Music in New York City. He accepted the Juilliard scholarship and, while taking a full course load there, picked up extra money by playing with the Brooklyn Philharmonic and in the pit orchestra for the Broadway musical *Sweeney Todd*. After a year at Juilliard, however, Marsalis began to feel that his versatility was being stifled. He later explained, "When you play jazz at Juilliard, people laugh; it's like the darkies cracking jokes, man."

This was not the first time he had felt what he called "racial vibes" at school. Although he was born in New Orleans, he had grown up and gone to school in the suburb of Kenner, which was primarily white. While he had been popular because of his musical talent, he had suspected that he would not have been as popular without it. He also felt that he had always been directed toward classical music as a more respectable form than jazz. So when Art Blakey, the famous black drummer, invited him to spend his 1980 summer vacation with his Jazz Messengers, Marsalis eagerly accepted. Soon, he was also the band's musical director. With Blakey, he began to attract attention from jazz critics.

The following year, Wynton Marsalis left Juilliard without taking a degree. He continued to play with Blakey from time to time but also toured Japan with jazz pianist Herbie Hancock's V.S.O.P. quartet. Hancock, his bassist Ron Carter, and his drummer Tony Williams had all been in the rhythm section of Miles Davis's band in the 1960s, and Wynton Marsalis learned much from them. He also made his first recordings with them, including the double album *Quartet* released by Columbia Records in 1981. In a *Down Beat* magazine poll for 1981, he was voted by jazz critics "the talent most deserving of wider recognition." That same year, Columbia Records gave him his own recording contract; the terms were unprecedented, for he was to record both jazz and classical music under that contract. His first album for Columbia, *Wynton Marsalis*, was produced by Herbie Hancock and included his older brother, Branford, on saxophone. Critics praised it, but remarked that it sounded very much like a Miles Davis album. Marsalis responded that "if you play trumpet and you *don't* sound like Miles or Dizzy [Gillespie] or Clifford [Brown] or Fats [Navarro], you're probably not playing jazz."

In 1981, Wynton formed his own jazz band with his brother Branford, Kenny Kirkland, Jeff Watts, Phil Bowler, and Ray Drummond. The band's first album, *Think of One*, was released by Columbia in 1983. Simultaneously, his first classical album, *Trumpet Concertos*, recorded in London with the National Philharmonic Orchestra, was released. Both sold more than one hundred thousand copies, which was unusual for either jazz or classical albums. Better yet, each album won a Grammy for Marsalis in February, 1984. His awards for best solo jazz instrumental performance and best classical performance with an orchestra by an instrumental soloist made him the first artist ever to win awards in both jazz and classical categories in a single year (in fact, no one before had ever even been nominated in both categories in a single year).

Still in his early twenties, Wynton Marsalis was a true musical phenomenon, for not only was he exceptionally talented in both classical and jazz music, but he also was enjoying the kind of high-powered marketing on the part of a major (white) label that few other black artists had. The advertising and marketing people at Columbia Records realized that what the critics were saying was true—because of his versatility, Wynton Marsalis brought a highly technical sense to his jazz playing and a vividness and immediacy to his classical playing that no one else had ever been able to do. Moreover, for one so young, he was remarkably articulate and outspoken, and he let it be known in no uncertain terms that he thought that jazz had been maligned too long as a kind of "noble savage" music that was too emotional to be viewed in the same light as classical music. Jazz, he said, was *more* difficult to play than classical music—more complicated, more technically demanding. By 1984, Marsalis was refusing to play jazz and classical music in the same program, and he had decided to concentrate on jazz, which he called "the ultimate twentieth-century music."

With the popular success of Wynton Marsalis, black American music has come full circle. In the early years when blacks were slaves, their own music was enjoyed and encouraged,

Wynton Marsalis was the first artist to be nominated for Grammy Awards in both jazz and classical categories in a single year. Not only was he nominated, but he also won both awards. He has said that jazz is more difficult to play than classical music.

(WIDE WORLD PHOTOS)

but not respected, by other Americans. The only black musicians who were successful were those who could sing or play European classical music. Over time, black music got "under the skin" of Americans to various degrees and began to influence the music of white Americans. By the middle of the twentieth century, most music experts agreed that jazz, a black music creation, was the only world musical style native to America. By the early 1980s, young Wynton Marsalis was stating that the most difficult white music (classical music from Europe) was less technically difficult than jazz (black music born in America). But he was not referring to technical difficulty when he called jazz the ultimate twentieth-century music. He was referring to a quality that is much harder to pin down.

Human beings make music because it somehow elevates them, causes them to rise up out of themselves, makes them feel better. In each period of history, in each place in the world, people have had different feelings and have responded to different kinds of music. In the twentieth century in America, it has been, and continues to be, black music or black-influenced music that makes the majority of music lovers feel better. And since, in the twentieth century, the rest of world tends to follow America's lead, it is the music that makes the world feel better.

As of this writing, black musicians and singers are still meeting with a lot of resistance. There are still radio stations that will not play black records, music videos shows that rarely feature black videos, and white record companies that spend less on promoting records by black artists than those by white artists. But very few people who know anything at all about music will pretend that twentieth-century American music is not heavily indebted to black music and black music makers. In fact, the influence of black music is now felt, and acknowledged, around the world.

SELECTED BIBLIOGRAPHY

Books

Abdul, Raoul. *Blacks in Classical Music.* New York: Dodd, Mead & Co., 1977.

Balliett, Whitney. *Jelly Roll, Jabbo & Fats: 19 Portraits in Jazz.* New York: Oxford University Press, 1983.

Charters, Samuel, and Leonard B. Kunstadt. *Jazz: A History of the New York Scene.* Garden City, N.Y.: Doubleday & Co., Inc., 1962.

Chilton, John. *Billie's Blues: The Billie Holiday Story 1933–1959.* Briarcliff Manor, N.Y.: Stein & Day, Publishers, 1975.

Courlander, Harold. *Negro Folk Music U.S.A.* New York: Columbia University Press, 1963.

Ferris, William T. *Blues From the Delta.* Garden City, N.Y.: Doubleday/Anchor Press, 1978.

Fox, Ted. *Showtime at the Apollo.* New York: Holt, Rinehart & Winston, 1983.

Gridley, Mark C. *Jazz Styles: History and Analysis,* 2nd ed. Englewood Cliffs, N.J.: Prentice-Hall, Inc., 1985.

Gutman, Bill. *Duke: The Musical Life of Duke Ellington.* New York: Random House, Inc., 1977.

Haskins, James. *About Michael Jackson.* Hillside, N.J.: Enslow Publishers, Inc., 1985.

———. *I'm Gonna Make You Love Me: The Story of Diana Ross.* New York: Dell Publishing Co., 1980.

———. *The Story of Stevie Wonder.* London: Granada Publishing Co., 1976.

Haskins, James, with Kathleen Benson. *Nat King Cole.* Briarcliff Manor, N.Y.: Stein & Day, Publishers, 1984.

———. *Scott Joplin: The Man Who Made Ragtime.* Briarcliff Manor, N.Y.: Stein & Day, Publishers, 1980.

Hirshey, Gerri. *Nowhere to Run: The Story of Soul Music.* New York: Times Books, 1984.

Jackson, Mahalia, with Evan McLeod Wylie. *Movin' On Up.* New York: Hawthorn Books, Inc., 1966.

Johnson, James Weldon. *Black Manhattan.* New York: Atheneum Publishers (reissue of a 1930 edition), 1968.

Katz, Bernard, ed. *The Social Implications of Early Negro Music in the United States.* New York: Arno/The New York Times, 1969.

Larkin, Rochelle. *Soul Music.* New York: Lancer Books, 1970.

Lieb, Sandra. *Mother of the Blues: A Study of Ma Rainey.*

Amherst, Mass.: University of Massachusetts Press, 1981.

Locke, Alain. *The Negro and His Music*. New York: Arno/ The New York Times (reissue of a 1936 edition), 1969.

Lomax, Alan. *Mr. Jelly Roll*. Berkeley: University of California Press, 1950.

Lovell, John, Jr. *Black Song: The Forge and the Flame*. New York: The Macmillan Company, 1972.

Parrish, Lydia. *Slave Songs of the Georgia Sea Islands*. Hatboro, Pa.: Folklore Associates, 1942.

Redding, Saunders. *They Came in Chains: Americans From Africa*. New York: J. B. Lippincott Co., 1950.

Southern, Eileen. *Biographical Dictionary of Afro-American and African Musicians*. Westport, Ct.: Greenwood Press, 1982.

————. *The Music of Black Americans: A History*. New York: W.W. Norton & Co., Inc., 1971.

Sterling, Dorothy, ed. *We Are Your Sisters: Black Women in the Nineteenth Century*. New York: W. W. Norton & Co., 1984.

Tirro, Frank. *Jazz: A History*. New York: W.W. Norton & Co., Inc., 1977.

Articles

Baraka, Amiri. "Miles Davis," *The New York Times Magazine* (June 16, 1985), pp. 24+.

Hinckley, David. "Crossing Over: A Story of Records and Race," *New York Daily News* (July 8, 1984), pp. 1+.

Holden, Stephen. "Rock Goes Back to the Future," *The New York Times* (July 26, 1985), pp. C1+.

Orth, Maureen. "Tina," *Vogue* (May 1985), pp. 318–319+.

"Quincy Jones," *Current Biography Yearbook* 1977, pp. 227–231.

"Wynton Marsalis," *Current Biography Yearbook* 1984, pp. 255–258.

Other Sources

Archives, Theatre and Music Collection, Museum of the City of New York.

Clippings files, New York Public Library for the Performing Arts, Lincoln Center.

Clippings files, New York Public Library, Schomburg Center for Research in Black Culture.

Interviews with Bo Diddley (1978) and Leontyne Price (1977).

INDEX